ANDREW SCHULZE

is nationally recognized as a Christian leader and pioneer in race relations. For over 30 years he served interracial parishes in St. Louis, Chicago, and Springfield, Ill. In 1954 he became the first executive secretary of the Lutheran Human Relations Association of America and joined the theological faculty of Valparaiso University.

By invitation of the late President John F. Kennedy the author participated in the White House Conference of Religious Leaders in 1963. In the same year he led an interracial goodwill tour of Europe. He has been active on civic and church commissions for race relations and wrote the book MY NEIGHBOR OF ANOTHER COLOR. In 1964 he became director of research for the LHRAA.

Fire from the Throne

FIRE FROM

THE THRONE

Race Relations in the Church

ANDREW SCHULZE

CONCORDIA PUBLISHING HOUSE
SAINT LOUIS LONDON

Concordia Publishing House, St. Louis, Missouri
Concordia Publishing House Ltd., London, E. C. 1

Library of Congress Catalog Card No. 68-21833

MANUFACTURED IN THE UNITED STATES OF AMERICA

To Margaret

Contents

Preface

At any given time there is no aspect of human existence that can be bypassed by the church if it is to fulfill its God-intended purpose in the world. The more complex society becomes, the greater the need for more knowledge about society—the world of human beings. The church must look to the sciences for such knowledge. To understand human beings as they are today in a convulsing world of revolutionary change—history, biology, anthropology, psychology, sociology, law, political science, and other branches of human learning can and must be the handmaiden of the church.

As the church employs the help of the sciences in relating its theology to the world—especially in a modern scientific age—it will discover that the Gospel has certain social implications. When theology speaks of man's relation to God and God's relation to man, there are always implications of man's relation to man. The ignoring or bypassing of the social implications of the Gospel by the church helped to give rise to Marxism, Leninism, and the now very generally repudiated social gospel of Walter Rauschenbusch. But the danger of bypassing the great thrust of Christian theology: God's relation to man and man's relation to God—while emphasizing man's relation to man—is still with us.

Between the covers of this book the reader will find page upon page devoted to the social implications of the Gospel as only the Gospel itself can speak to man in relation to his fellowman in a world of growing impersonal automation. But the church has a higher goal than social reform. In serving man, God is to be served. God's exaltation and glory are the ultimate purpose of Christian theology and of the church to whom the Word of God has been entrusted. God is not merely to be used as a helpful Father in the interest of His needy children, but the needy children are to be helped because of God, His will, and His glory. If the real purpose of this book is to be understood, the book as a whole must be seen from the perspective of man's relation to man in and through the reconciliation of God to man and man to God through Christ.

Many of the illustrations, anecdotes, and references have come out of the author's own church-denomination experience; however, the church as spoken of in the book is no specific denomination, but rather all Christian churches in the United States, and specifically the so-called white church—unless the so-called Negro church is specified.

The theology herein developed is in the main basic to that to which the major church bodies subscribe; it is drawn from the Scriptures of the Old and New Testaments and confessed in the great ecumenical creeds. The strengths and weaknesses of the several major denominations as they address themselves to the race issue are largely very similar.

Among church people in all major denominations and in all sections of our land, a great lack of understanding is still to be found of the real nature of the race issue, of the theology that addresses itself to the issue, and of the true character of the church's involvement or noninvolvement in the issue. The uninformed are also found among clergy and laity who in other areas are well informed and who have a sincere concern for what is right and good and Christian. It is to them primarily that this book addresses itself.

Although reference is made occasionally to racial and ethnic minorities other than Negroes, the text centers the reader's attention on Negroes for two related reasons: They are our largest minority group—more than 90 percent of our so-called nonwhite population; and Negro-white relations are the great concern of millions of our citizens, while the smaller groups of nonwhite minorities are the direct concern of a proportionately smaller percentage of our population. But it must be stressed that the ethical and theological principles involved apply to all; they are as universal in their application as the universality of the human species.

All Scripture texts used, if not otherwise indicated, are from the Revised Standard Version.

Foreword

This book by Dr. Andrew Schulze of Valparaiso University fills a great and real need. It covers a wide range of problems all related to the basic problem of race. The author properly says that this question is undoubtedly the most vexing part of our future, especially since it involves the worldwide population explosion. The number of human beings on this planet increases by 7,000 an hour; of these 5,000 are nonwhite, non-Christian, and non-Western.

Among the subjects which the author touches in his examination of the entire question are the rise of nationalism, the sociological—not biological—"nature of race," the American dilemma, fundamentalism, communism, wars and their effect on the tangled situation.

It is inevitable that there is fire and passion in this book. How can it be otherwise? We have here a long history of wrong, the story of the plundered and the poor, the tale of world tragedy and national trauma. It regularly rises to the surface of public affairs and reflects the now uneasy, now self-righteous, seldom relevant and concerned, attitude of our postmodern world. It is only recently that brave crusaders and friends of nonwhite man have broken through the hard surface of our consciousness.

This book represents an unusually sharp and intelligent survey of the entire situation. There are, of course (that is to be expected), a few evidences of special pleading. Not all readers will be able to accept completely the author's curt dismissal of the white college student. His approach may not be the whole story of the relationship of white and black on our American campuses. Some may think that the abuses of black power are occasionally glossed over, although the author points out the weaknesses of this movement.

Dr. Schulze's approach is dominated by a single sentence which he writes at the beginning of the book: "We are moving faster day by day toward a totally different tomorrow which no one can fully foresee." This acceptance of the ambiguity and uncertainty of the future must certainly be basic in our approach to the problems which the author considers so eloquently. We cannot see the end from the beginning.

Particularly valuable for the Christian student of social affairs are the chapters on the theological truths which must be applied to the civil rights problem. This is, after all, the heart of the matter.

The author's examination of the theological undergirding of his position is relevant and consistent. He points both to the doctrine of creation and the meaning of the new creation in Christ. These are discussed perceptively and sensitively. The new life, the author notes, is centered in Christ—in His resurrection and the resultant *agape* by which our Lord works through us. Here is an accurate reflection of the great divine discontinuity of history in Jesus Christ. His discussion of the resulting two kingdoms is most relevant.

Particularly interesting is Dr. Schulze's honest discussion of the problems of interracial marriage. He emphasizes correctly that there are no theological problems involved here and that interracial marriage is theologically valid. On the other hand, he points out that under present circumstances it is probably not desirable. This recognition of the ideal and the real is characteristic of the author's entire approach to the race question.

The position of the author in the civil rights movement is, of course, well known. Not only with his work but with his life he has demonstrated his complete and devoted commitment to the righting of the wrongs which the black man has suffered these many centuries.

This book will be an excellent tool in the hands of the pastor who wishes to instruct his parish in some of the principles and problems involved in the fundamental question. Under the leadership of men like Dr. Schulze the church has begun to do much better in confronting the harsh realities of the situation, but there is still room for great improvement. The organization of discussion groups using this book as a basis should be a powerful factor in bringing all sections of the institutional church to a greater and deeper realization of their duties and opportunities in this important field. The author has performed a very real service to the Church Militant—in which there is finally no white or black.

O. P. Kretzmann
President, Valparaiso University

The Feast of the Epiphany of our Lord, 1968

Acknowledgements

The author is indebted to Valparaiso University and its president, Dr. O. P. Kretzmann, for a stipend from the Committee on Creative Work and Research and for a semester's leave from teaching responsibilities; to the Lutheran Human Relations Association of America for a year's freedom from executive responsibilities; to the Wheat Ridge Foundation for its grant to LHRAA which helped make the leave possible, and for its awareness of the interrelated significance of racial injustice to health and welfare problems as well as missionary opportunity; to the Committee on Research of The Lutheran Church – Missouri Synod; to my colleagues, Karl E. Lutze, Edward H. Schroeder, Anne Springsteen, and John Strietelmeier; to other persons too numerous to mention, including many people throughout the country and the church who gave encouragement through expressed convictions and commitment; and to my wife, who by her moral support and self-effacing labor, especially her assistance in research and in typing and retyping, helped to make the book possible. While these lines are intended as an expression of grateful acknowledgement of all the cooperation and assistance given, the responsibility for the weaknesses that the discerning reader will detect in the book is solely that of the author.

Valparaiso, Ind.

1

Racism and Race

The ancient problems of man seem most visibly represented today in things racial.[1]

Racism Since Time Immemorial

Like the poor and sin, we shall always have racism with us. Though it may appear in a somewhat different form in each new age, it is always there to plague human society; more accurately stated, human society plagues itself with racism. It has been traced through the historical development of the human inhabitants of every continent, including North, Central, and South America.

By means of modern European imperialism and colonialism, peoples of Asia and Africa were exploited. They were shorn of their sovereignty, their lands, their natural resources, or of an unhappy combination of all three. Since this kind of racism is still in existence in some places and vivid in the minds of those who in recent years have gained their freedom, it is understandable that this modern form of racism is in the dead center of the present worldwide race issue, while that of former ages is unknown or forgotten.

If history is to a large extent a record of man's treatment of man or of one group taking advantage of another, it would appear obvious that, unless the nature of man is changed, we would be living in a fool's paradise to believe that we are now suddenly going to change the face of the earth and rid it of racism. The poor, sin, and racism are still with us, and they probably will be in the future. But having said that, we would not argue against Marx, Lenin, or their successors for planning to get rid of poverty—though their total ideology may be another matter—nor oppose the Federal Government in its purpose expressed in the antipoverty program enacted into law in August 1964. Neither would we argue against the preacher for denouncing sin and working against it. Similarly, we cannot reject legitimate endeavors to fight racism. In the second half of the 20th century, every sinew of our political and ecclesiastical being must be employed to fight any racism that raises its ugly head.

If racism of past ages was a menace to society—and it surely was—today it can become the element in society that may touch off the emotional spark that will annihilate not only civilization but humanity itself. To work at its eradication is no longer a convenient pastime intended to fill in otherwise dull moments of leisure; nor can it be the activity of the isolated reformer who is merely tolerated by the rest of society. Too long has the eradication of racism been the concern of professionals whose learned volumes now grace the shelves of university libraries in ever-increasing numbers, sparking an occasional student reaction irritating to those who would maintain the status quo, but doing nothing beyond that to the masses of people—of politicians and preachers and pew-warmers.

Live Together or Die Together

The racism briefly described as the heritage of the past affected comparatively small sections of humanity: a tribe fighting against a tribe or a nation against a nation or, at worst, an Alexander, a Caesar, or a Genghis Khan sweeping a path of misery, destruction, and death over a thousand or more miles but leaving ninety-nine percent of the earth's surface untouched and undisturbed. Now there is no alternative; it is either—or. Men will either learn to live together or they will surely die together. In a more literal sense than that intended by the prophet Isaiah (2:4), swords must be beaten into plowshares and spears into pruning hooks. The destructive power of nuclear weapons is well known, and more powerful ones are being developed so fast that by the time a sizable number of one description have been manufactured they are made obsolete by new and more powerful ones.

Provocative Incidents but No War

There have been many incidents since World War II which, in the days of the sword and the spear, gunpowder and cannon, would have erupted into a war of bloodletting involving all the military power at the disposal of both sides. But these incidents have not had that result since 1945. International incidents have disturbed nerves and caused tensions to mount, with brush-fire wars breaking out here and there, but they have not led to another world war. Among the more constructive things that have happened are the signing in 1963 of the Nuclear Test Ban Treaty, the establishment of the "hot line" between Moscow and Washington (which was kept busy during the 1967 Arab-Israeli war), and the unprecedented existence over two decades of an international political body, the United Nations, a world forum intended primarily to keep the peace.

Must one draw the conclusion that our present-day government authorities, with the power at their disposal to plunge their nations and the nations of the world into war, are more moral or ethical than the Caesars, the Alexanders, the Bismarcks, the Kaisers, and the kings of ages and decades now past? Perhaps some are and some are not. They are quite obviously restraining themselves because they know full well not only that both sides would be losers but that all-out war would mean total destruction of friend and foe. It should therefore be evident that, if the world is to survive, men will have to learn somehow to live together.

But the banning of nuclear tests and honest total disarmament alone will not prove to be the panacea that will turn this earth, pockmarked on every continent by the wars of tribes and nations and empires, into a heavenly paradise. We must take into consideration other factors that make the world in which we are now living quite different from that of the age of any of our forebears. The earth's growing population is one of them.

People in the Billions a Factor

From the time of man's origin on earth, according to Robert C. Cook, president of Population Reference Bureau, it took until the year 1800 "for world population to reach the billion mark. . . . In the intervening 166 years, world population more than tripled. So rapid has the acceleration in growth been that, as matters now stand, the next doubling will occur around the end of the century and the population would increase to more than 9 billion in about 50 years. The United Nations estimates that world population is now growing by 2 percent per year. At this rate, population doubles in 35 years, and in a century it increases nearly eightfold. In 2066, the total would be 24 billion."[2] If this trend continues—and authorities until now have no practical suggestions as to how it can be changed—where will people live, and what will be the source of an adequate food supply?

Among those countries and continents which have been called the "haves"—Europe, Soviet Russia, the United States, and Canada—the population increase during the period of modern growth has been the least, and it is estimated their increase until the year 2000 will be the least; while among those countries and continents which have been called the "have-nots," whose people live in poverty and near starvation all their lives, the population increase has been and will continue to be the greatest. Millions are without shelter adequate for comfort, health, or even existence.

The immediate concern of this book, though, is that by and large the "haves" are the whites, and the "have-nots" are the so-called colored peoples of the world—some two billion of them. The percentage of the white world population is decreasing day by day, and conversely the percentage of nonwhites is increasing. "Of the 220 babies born in the world per minute, over half arrive in Asia." [3]

Race and the Worldwide Nationalist Movement

If race were not an element in the thinking of whites and nonwhites, the ratio of whites to nonwhites now and in the coming decades could be a matter of complete indifference. But we are living in a world that has been influenced throughout the centuries of human history by racism of one type or another. The humiliation of the slavery of the past few centuries, in which the dominant whites enslaved the Africans, cannot be easily forgotten. The colonialism and imperialism of the immediate past to a great degree prevented the free economic and political development of the peoples of Asia and Africa and on the other hand enriched the dominant European Caucasians and helped to develop in them an attitude of arrogant superiority.

If all these factors were not present to influence men's thinking and actions, race, the color of man's skin, and all the other superficial biological traits would be of little consequence, and race would not be a determining factor in the dangerous decades into which the world is moving. But in spite of all that the theologians, the social scientists, and the statesmen can do, the colored peoples will be thinking about race and the part it has played in the past; and the once-dominant whites are and perhaps will be most reluctant, even with all the facts in the case against them, to quit thinking in color and to eliminate their prejudices, whether they be of a racial or ethnic type.

A life-and-death struggle is going on between the two great military and political powers of the world, the United States, and the communist powers now centered in Moscow and Peking. But there is another power with which both of these must contend and which in the end can turn the balance of power in one direction or another. That is the power of the so-called uncommitted nations —in the main those nations which through the rise of nationalism have already gained their independence and those who will have theirs before long: all of them nonwhite peoples.

A source of serious embarrassment to the United States in its approach to these nations is among other things our alliance in NATO with those political entities from whom, after a long and bitter struggle, these new nations have gained their independence. Still other nations or peoples are working to gain their freedom from our allies. Both the White House and the Pentagon, if not Congress, must be conscious of this dilemma in which we as a nation find ourselves; and the desperate need for improved race relations at home does not lessen our predicament.

The revival of interest in and the development of non-Christian religions in lands where a new nationalism is gaining independence for its people is not altogether coincidental. At least in some places it is a tool in the hands of the nationalist leaders to unify their people and to give them identity so that the new political structure which is emerging will be recognized as their own and a solidarity will develop among them without which no revolutionary government could survive. The decline of Christianity in these nonwhite countries may have serious political repercussions.

A discussion of the worldwide race issue as treated thus far is intended to help find a satisfactory world perspective for a particular facet of the issue. What is happening in race relations in the United States cannot be properly understood nor dealt with effectively with hope of change for the better unless it is seen in the perspective of race relations throughout the world. And race relations in this country, whether good or bad, affect the well-being of the church here at home as well as our nation with respect to the unity of its component parts. Since, however, the nation, with the church in it, is not an island to itself but a part of and interrelated and interdependent with the whole complex world of our day, our national race relations affect the life and activity of the church, especially in its world outreach; and our race relations affect every detail of our relations with other nations, primarily of course with the new, emerging, independent nations whose peoples are nonwhite.

The Bad Word "Race"

A definition of race is hard to come by, if one desires an accurate description of human beings in keeping with the best of scientific research. Scientists differ greatly in defining race; and some would remove the term entirely from our vocabulary.[4] Human beings are with us still, and (despite the difficulty in clearly categorizing them) they have a tendency to appear on the earth's surface with differing physical traits, such as skin color and hair texture.

> It is a common fallacy to assume that the peoples of the world can be divided into two or three clearly defined racial groups on the basis of skin color alone. The simple dichotomy of "white" and "colored," and the threefold classification into black or negroid, white or caucasoid, and yellow or mongoloid, have assumed a certain social significance, but they do not correspond with geneticists' understanding of racial differences. . . . The inhabitants of Africa and Asia range from a pale yellow to a very dark brown.[5]

It is fairly safe to say that if the race concept is to be employed at all (and that within the limits of reliable scientific research), it must be "confined to such physical characteristics as stature, color of skin, hair and eyes, shape of head, nose and lips, cross section of hair, and blood grouping."[6] That's all. Nothing more.

Why, then, is more ignorance found within one racial group in a given area than another? Or why does one find a greater degree of delinquency and criminality, for example, in our Negro ghettos of New York, Chicago, and other metropolitan centers than one finds among the whites of those cities? Scientists tell us there are two things that determine man's being: nature and nurture. The physical traits mentioned are attributable to nature or to the genes inherited from one's ancestors. Innate intelligence, too, is an inherited trait, but this inheritance is not limited to a given race or races. Without the influence of certain environmental factors—nurture—some persons are more intelligent than others, but even this distinction is not racial. Some members of one race are innately more intelligent than others of the same race. For example, some Caucasians are innately more intelligent than other Caucasians. Some Negroes are innately less intelligent than other Negroes, but some Negroes are also innately more intelligent than some Caucasians, and vice versa.

Aside from the inheritance factor, which in the matter of intelligence level does not follow racial lines at all, it may be safe to say that as far as scientists have been able to determine, ignorance or intelligence as well as all forms of social, moral, and ethical behavior are determined by environment or nurture. How a man talks; how he acts under given circumstances; whether he becomes a drunkard, a robber, or a confidence man; or whether he becomes a useful citizen and an asset to society, depends, within the limitations already defined, on nurture or environment—not on skin pigmentation, hair texture, or any or all of the physical traits that characterize the racial group with which he is identified. Ministers and social workers and others who have had opportunity over an extended period of time to visit the homes of people who are compelled to live in underprivileged, blighted sections of our big cities can testify to the integrity of many, perhaps the majority, of the people living there. Despite the odds against them in the form of unfavorable community living conditions, they maintain a high standard of moral conduct.

Many scientists accept the theory that man had a common origin. Perhaps equally widespread among scientists is the theory that there are three major racial groups, the Negroid, the Caucasoid, and the Mongoloid. The purest of the Negroid race are found in central west Africa, the purest Mongoloids in eastern China, and the purest Caucasians in northern Europe.[7] But having said this, one must hasten to add that beyond a very small portion of each of these racial groups, the great masses of people inhabiting the earth are "purely" human, neither Negroid, Caucasoid, nor Mongoloid. If there ever were "pure races," they have disappeared as a result of untold generations of commingling. Where people have lived together for thousands of years, racial purity as an existing phenomenon is a pure myth. This applies especially to the Mediterranean countries, and to Europe where the modern myth of racial superiority was born not long ago, where it blossomed during Nazism and from which part of the globe it has been greedily borrowed by others, especially by the Republic of South Africa, with its presently developing and precarious apartheid system, and by the United States of America, particularly in the South.

A further potent and quite obvious argument upholding the theory that the human family is one, and showing that any attempt to maintain a pure racial stock is farcical, is the somewhat recent discovery of basic blood types. Some 1,900 years ago St. Paul said that God "hath made of one blood all nations of men for to dwell on all the face of the earth." (Acts 17:26 KJV)

What "Negro" Means

For all practical purposes, the term "Negro" as it is used in our society is a sociological, not a biological, term; we are white or we are Negro in keeping with the group with which we are identified. "The social definition of 'Negro' may be expressed as: 'Everyone having a *known* trace of Negro blood in his veins,' no matter how far back it was acquired. Thus, *the social definition is dependent upon community knowledge of racial ancestry, with or without physical racial visibility*"[8] (emphasis added). An interesting example of this type of racial classification is found in Lillian Smith's *Killers of the Dream,* in which she describes a childhood experience. One of the ladies in her mother's club told her friends that she had seen a little white girl living with a Negro family in the community. Soon thereafter the clubwomen, escorted by the town marshal, took the child from her adopted family and brought her to Lillian's home. The two girls became deeply attached to each other. Some weeks later, after a club meeting at the Smith home, it was decided that the child was Negro, and she was forthwith returned to "Colored Town."[9]

Passing for White

Passing for white is the result of the determination of a person previously identified with the Negro community as a Negro to lose such identification and in doing so to become "white." To effect this change the person must burn all bridges behind him. Usually, he moves to another city or state, and every possible step is taken to disassociate himself from former acquaintances and friends. Passing is undertaken not necessarily because the person doing it is ashamed of being Negro, but rather to avoid the unfortunate discrimination which an unfriendly society heaps upon those identified as Negroes as though such identification were a sure mark of inferiority. The effect of the color bar in American society is reflected in the reluctance of many dark Puerto Ricans to learn English.

Passing has been going on for a long time; nevertheless, the trend is decreasing and probably will continue to do so. Estimates of the number of negroes who pass annually into white society range from a few thousands to tens of thousands.

In the early days of our history, when white women were scarce, in some states, e. g., Louisiana, white men freely mixed their blood with that of the Negro. They gave their genes to Negro women not only in extramarital relations but also through interracial marriage, which was permitted and even encouraged in some areas. The Negro historian and Pittsburgh *Courier* columnist J. A. Rogers claims to have documented evidence that many of the Southern segregationist leaders in state governments are descendants of persons who in our earlier history found their entrance into life through miscegenation.

Despite all the light that careful, objective scientific research and study shed on the question of race and despite the experience of man throughout his generations, teaching him that racism is an evil ultimately helping no one and only bringing misery and woe upon him and his fellowman, race—which is a helpful, wholesome phenomenon of nature—is often used by man to his own grief and disgrace. The history of our nation is a glaring example of it. Race relations in the United States have been and still are contrary to sound morality and ethics and to the best ideology written into the Declaration of Independance and the Constitution.

2

1619 to 1930, and Beyond

Every one to whom much is given, of him will much be required.

Luke 12:48

There were Negro slaves in what is now called South Carolina, formerly a Spanish colony. But slavery was not long-lived there; the slaves revolted and fled to the Indians. The history of Negroes in English America had its origin with the landing at Jamestown, Va., in August 1619 of "twenty negars." Slavery was at that time nonexistent in the colonies. Since there was no established pattern of chattel slavery as found in other lands, the 20 Africans became indentured servants. It wasn't long, though, before the colonies caught on. Statutory recognition was given to slavery in Massachusetts in 1641, in Connecticut in 1650, in Virginia in 1661, in Maryland in 1662, in New York and New Jersey in 1664, in South Carolina in 1684, Rhode Island and Pennsylvania in 1700, North Carolina in 1725, and Georgia in 1750.

Approximately half a million slaves were in the colonies when our national forefathers affixed their names to a document called the Declaration of Independence, in which they—many of them slaveholders themselves—said in evident sincerity and for the most part in Christian piety: "All men are created equal . . . they are endowed by their Creator with certain unalienable rights . . . among these are life, liberty, and the pursuit of happiness." But even before the Revolutionary War there were formal protests against slavery, made by Quakers and others. The picture projected by some popular volumes on American history and until recently accepted by many was that Negro slaves and later their descendants were a docile people and, for all practical purposes, happy with their lot. It may come as a shock to some to learn the true facts of our history: that there were many slave revolts from pre-Revolutionary days to the time of the Civil War, one as early as 1712, when in New York 9 whites were killed and 21 slaves were executed.

Not long after the Revolutionary War, slavery was banned from the Northern states, but with cotton becoming the king of the Southern economy, the slave system developed into a firmly entrenched institution in the South.

The Church in the South

One would suppose that when the inhuman master-slave society took on form in the early days of our nation's history, the church, undergirded by Biblical theology, would have been in the vanguard in opposing such a system, especially in view of the claim so often made that Christianity gave the death knell to slavery in the pagan Roman Empire. But the church did not measure up to that standard. It did not demonstrate in its life the revolutionary spirit of its Lord and of those who became His first witnesses in a pagan world. Not only that. It could be anticipated or at least hoped that if the church did not have the will to wage all-out warfare on the master-slave way of life, it would at least have remained impassive—bad as that is in itself. Some say that the early church overthrew the slave system in the Roman Empire not by a frontal attack upon the system but by the introduction into society of a new concept of what constitutes a good society. But the church in the South was neither aggressively antislavery, nor merely impassive or neutral. The church was part of the whole cultural milieu in which the master-slave tradition was formed and made fast until the time of the Civil War and the Emancipation Proclamation.

What the Southern church did or did not do was determined by the specific time involved and the status of the economic and cultural trends of that time; for example, before the Revolutionary War, at the time of the expansion of the cotton plantation system, when slave traffic was outlawed, and when the full impact of Northern antislavery activity was felt. As an institution the church was always involved in what was happening in the society of which it was a part.

What is abundantly clear and evident throughout the antebellum period is the interrelatedness between what the church did—or did not do—and what, according to the leaders in the church, was demanded of the church in the interest of the economic and cultural stability of the community and of the South in general. The Christian religion was to be brought to the slaves, but its teachings were to be slanted toward what was considered helpful in maintaining a master-slave society and a white-supremacy-oriented economic and cultural stability.

Even within the framework of a strong master-slave society, there was at times during the antebellum days some freedom for the slaves in the Southern church in its educational and worship program. But this freedom was vigorously resisted later.

At times the slaves worshiped in the same church building and in the same worship service with whites—the slaves also participating with them in the Lord's Supper. There are examples, too, of Negroes acting as pastors of white congregations. It was thought better to allow the slaves to worship with them than to have them meet separately where insurrection against slavery could more easily be fostered.[1]

The acceptance of slaves into the life and fellowship of the church was always within the pattern of a master-slave society. When such fellowship was seen to threaten the system, it was not tolerated.

Making the tenets of the Christian religion known to the slaves was very generally considered a necessary part of the master-slave way of life. It served several purposes. The masters themselves, perhaps with some exceptions, were members and in many cases pillars of the church. They were continually confronted with the Christian responsibility to witness to Christ and to teach the precepts of the faith. To neglect doing so, even in the case of the slaves, would unduly disturb their conscience.

There were other very practical reasons for teaching the doctrines of the Christian faith to the slaves. It would help to establish a better image of themselves in the eyes of their detractors from the North, many of whom, motivated by their Christian profession, opposed the slave system. Furthermore, it was thought that the Christianization of the slaves would make better slaves of them. They would learn to be obedient to their masters. They would develop many Christian virtues, such as kindliness, love, patience, and diligence. They would become lovers of peace. But above all they would be reconciled to their lowly estate, if not happy in it, by the knowledge and hope of a happy hereafter in heaven.

Of necessity other emphases which help to make Christianity what it truly is—equality, justice, liberty, freedom, the responsibility to recognize one's God-given talents and to use them freely for the common good without the restraint imposed by a dehumanizing denial of one's total humanity—all these emphases were not for the slave, unless in some way he could understand them as his possession in the hereafter.

In the Republic of South Africa today many of the politically powerful men are leading members of the dominant church of that country. Not unlike them, the leading citizens of our South, under the master-slave system, looked to the church, its Bible, its doctrines, and its ministers for justification of the master-slave system that would be respectable for a Christian-oriented society; and in most instances they got what they were looking for. The major doctrines of the Christian faith, beginning with the creation and ending with the bliss of heaven, were so slanted as to make Christianity a caricature of its real self.[2]

AS THE CHURCH DUG ITSELF OUT OF THE DEBRIS

The Civil War, the Emancipation Proclamation, the Reconstruction Period, and the Thirteenth, Fourteenth, and Fifteenth Amendments removed the foundation; the master-slave society was no more. If that way of life had been the result merely of an ungodly secular society into which the church of the South had been thrust, somewhat similar to the pagan society in which the primitive church in the days of the apostles had to operate, the status of the Southern church as it dug itself out of the debris of those traumatic years would have been quite different. But that was not the case. The Southern church was an integral part of the origin, development, and protection of the master-slave society. The church gave to that society a religious undergirding. To take away the master-slave relationship from society was robbing the church of its religion, for the church knew quite well that the Christian religion has a horizontal as well as a vertical dimension. But the church had planned and constructed the horizontal to fit neatly into the framework of a society which after the war no longer existed. In other words, its whole religious structure was lying in ruins after the war. For that reason it was totally unprepared psychologically and theologically to lead its people and Southern society when that society needed its help most.

At the end of the war a pall of frustration settled upon the South. When it began to lift, with Reconstruction past and Federal troops recalled, the South began to look among the shambles for something of the past that could be salvaged. The master-slave society as such was gone forever. But the South began to pick up some of its pieces. When they were put together, though made out of the same old stuff, all the system had which resembled its past was white supremacy.

The former slaves were not to be excluded from that society; if they had been, who would have remained to do the work? They were a part of the South, but they were to know their place, and daily they were to be reminded of their inferiority and the supremacy of those called white. The white South after the war remained a deeply religious community. It needed a religious undergirding for its culture. And so the assumed inferiority of the Negroes as well as the assumed superiority of the white man became an article of faith, a natural evolution of its historic past.[3]

The antebellum society was a master-slave society; the postbellum society was to be white-supremacy structured according to something somewhat new, segregation. But both were to serve the same end: the proponents of the two systems wanted to save themselves. The supremacists were to exploit those considered inferior. Under segregation as well as under slavery all things were to work together for the good of them that are called white.

As the church had been a partner in the building of the old, so now it became the co-worker with the society in which it found its existence and moulded that new society out of the salvaged materials which its own leaders had helped to place into the framework of the old.

The new postbellum Southern way of life did not appear, hocus-pocus-like, well-developed and fully accepted, with the waving of a magic wand. Segregation was rather slow in coming. It was not until after the Plessy-Ferguson Supreme Court decision of 1896 that segregation became the overall pattern.[4] From the time of the close of the war until Plessy-Ferguson, while the South was still groping about without a generally established and accepted new cultural pattern, there was placed before the door of the church of the South the golden opportunity to become the conscience of society and to lead in moulding it according to a pattern of justice and equity that would embrace both former masters and former slaves. But instead of calling upon the people, Joshua-like, to go forward courageously to the promised land of milk and honey, the church in the South looked back longingly to the fleshpots of Egypt; it helped salvage out of the ashes of the old system something that would help build a society as nearly approximating the old as time and circumstance would permit: the church helped in the establishment of the segregation system.

During those dark days of United States history, the always imminent danger of lynching hung like an ominous pall over the Negro community. The effect of lynchings on Negroes in the South was like that of the Gestapo in Nazi Germany stopping at a house and taking its inhabitants to Auschwitz or Buchenwald. But lynching was not an isolated idiosyncrasy in the behavior of that region of our land. It was not the sum total of all that was evil in the system. It was rather symbolical of the many evils that daily surrounded the lives of Negroes. Lynching was a bold reminder to all adult Negroes of what any infraction of the segregation system could bring upon them at any moment of their lives.

At least the better element of Southern church people could no doubt say with a degree of honesty and satisfaction that they would not hurt or harm their Negro neighbors, that lynchings and other acts of violence committed against Negroes were the deeds of a lunatic fringe in the society. But every open or subtle approval of segregation involved these church people. It helped to establish in their own minds as well as in the minds of others that whiteness is a badge of superiority established by Him who in creation has made a skin-color distinction. Hence every violation of segregation was a violation of the moral code and robbed those that are called white of their God-given prerogative of superiority; and those who tried to violate the inviolable deserved to suffer and to receive the due reward of their deeds.

Before the Civil War (during the days of slavery) and after the Civil War (during the days of the development of the segregation system) the South was deeply religious. The church was the center of community life. It taught and established the morals and ethics of the community. The church of the South was a Bible-believing church. The major tenets of the faith as expressed in the Ecumenical Creeds of Christendom were the doctrinal foundation on which the church's teaching and preaching were based. These doctrines were confessed with the lips: the Trinity, the deity of Christ, the Virgin Birth, the vicarious atonement through the death and resurrection of Christ, and the Bible as the norm of Christian faith and life. But in spite of its profession, the church became the exponent of morals and ethics that were inimical to the faith it professed.[5]

When one considers what the church had in its professed teaching and how it used such teaching to foster and support at first a master-slave society and later a system of racial segregation, the words of Jesus spoken as a judgment upon the religious leaders of His day seem to apply: "The last state of that man becomes worse than the first" (Luke 11:26). Inhumanity, such as was inherent in slavery and racial segregation, is wicked when fostered by those making no profession of religion, but when practiced in the name of religion such inhumanity becomes seven times more wicked.[6]

With the historical background of the church in the South until the thirties as described above, one might have some inkling about the reaction of its members to the earth-shaking changes soon to take place. The statements on race relations by the Oxford Conference in 1937 hardly caused a ripple in the church on the local level in the South; neither did the Supreme Court decisions in the Gaines, Sweatt, and Sipuel cases, all calling for the admission of Negroes to Southern schools of higher learning. The decision of the Court in 1948 declaring neighborhood restrictive covenants unenforceable in courts of law might have been noticed by Southern church people, merely evoking an expression about their stone-throwing Yankee neighbors, without touching them at any vital point in their lives as Christians and church members. Even President Truman's executive order calling for desegregation of the armed forces did not affect them too greatly; most of their sons had been unscathed in World War II and untouched by Negro nearness overseas. The integration of the armed forces was disliked by Southerners, but it did not necessarily affect their own lives sufficiently to disturb them. At least in their church life they remained unchanged; segregation continued. "A Baptist layman in Virginia, who had just returned from the 1957 State Convention of the Defenders of State Sovereignty and Individual Liberties . . . said . . . 'Sooner or later, school integration is sure to come—*but we still have the church.* Negroes will never take that over.'"[7]

The Northern Church

During the decades immediately preceding the Civil War, the North became the great exponent of freedom for the slaves. After the war, at least for a time, the North was the champion of equal rights for the freedmen. As the North went, so went the church in the North. As the battle lines between the two geographic areas became more clearly defined, the lines of separation in the church, too, became more and more fixed. Three major Protestant denominations with large Southern constituencies, the Methodists, the Baptists, and the Presbyterians, were split and formed independent Northern and Southern bodies.

Under these conditions there was no suffering for Christ involved in the Northern church's witness against slavery and, after the war, against the child and heir of slavery—white supremacy. With the political atmosphere prevailing at the time, the church could witness against slavery and later against segregation without the danger of community opposition; in fact, the church could anticipate community and political approval of its stand.

After the holocaust of the war, with its impoverishment of the South, the freedmen were out in a cold and ruthless world, on their own, having to shift for themselves, without property and education and without a fixed cultural pattern so necessary for the security of any people. Many of the churches in the North recognized the plight of Southern Negroes, and some of them addressed themselves to the Negro's needs, especially in the field of education.

A very discernible attitude soon developed, that of bypassing the basic need of the acceptance of the freedmen as human beings in human society; and this attitude was conditioned in many cases by a conservative theology which de-emphasized both the human need and the means for meeting it: "Just preach the Gospel; that will take care of everything." E. g.: A federation of five Lutheran church bodies, called the Evangelical Lutheran Synodical Conference of North America, came into existence in 1872. In 1877 they resolved to begin missionary work among Negroes. Much missionary zeal and personal sacrifice went into this work, so that at the turn of the century churches and Christian day schools had been established in New Orleans and other parts of Louisiana, in Virginia, and North and South Carolina. In 1916 this work was begun in the Black Belt of Alabama, where many churches and day schools sprang up throughout the rural area of the central part of that state. This group and others of different denominations worked hard at their task but apparently oversimplified their responsibility. Those responsible for the conduct of this work avoided tackling the issues of human dignity and human rights. In their missionary zeal and perhaps confronted with the opposition of white supremacists, they did not minister to the total need of the total man.

There were other historic developments which helped to rationalize the ministry to the souls of men while bypassing other basic, known human needs.

When concerned people in the North and the South were looking for an easy solution to the racial problem, a Negro prophet arose. His message was accepted by many as an oracle from heaven. In a speech at the Atlanta fair in 1895, Booker T. Washington, who was already considered by many the greatest Negro leader of that day, said: "In all things that are purely social, we can be as separate as the fingers, yet one as the hand in all things essential to mutual progress." That was easy: separate but equal. Separate in all things social, but equal in all things economic. It did not take much imagination to make the application to the life and work of the church: civil rights is a social, not a theological, matter.

At about the turn of the century there were two concomitant historical developments that were to help establish the race-relations climate prevalent throughout the land in the thirties when the race issue began to emerge. In 1896 the Plessy-Ferguson decision of "separate but equal" was handed down by the Supreme Court, giving to the fast-developing segregation system status and legal acceptance. At the same time circumstances were developing on our little neighbor island to the south, Cuba, that were to make of us—whether we wanted it or not—an empire. These circumstances climaxed in 1898 in the sinking of the *Maine* and the beginning of the Spanish-American War. The result: we, instead of the Spanish, assumed sovereignty over Cuba, Puerto Rico, the Philippines, and other small Spanish island possessions; and the segregation thought pattern with its assumed and often-expressed white superiority became a convenient model for our relationship with our little brown brothers who had now become a part of our political family.

With the simultaneous impact of the developing segregation pattern and the subtle infiltration into our society of a spirit of Western imperialism, the church in the North, living within this environmental climate, could do but one of two things: resist or succumb. The history of the succeeding several decades, however, does not demonstrate that the church in the North caused its voice to be heard in defense of a universal human brotherhood which would at every turn challenge both segregation and imperialism.

THE CHURCH IN PANIC

Toward the end of the fourth decade of this century, many sweeping changes began to be felt in our society which affected white and Negro relationships as nothing in our previous history.

These changes also affected the church, disturbing its surface complacency. One such change was the great population shift—Negroes moving from the South to the North and West. Literally hundreds of the biggest churches in all the major church denominations in the inner city of Detroit, New York, Philadelphia, Cleveland, Chicago, and Los Angeles were now faced with the opportunity to prove that the people to whom their pastors were preaching held no attitude of race prejudice inimical to their Christian profession. Now there were new people moving into the community who needed everything good that the church had to offer. But when the Negroes moved in, white church members moved out. The trek to the outlying districts and the suburbs, begun by church members, was soon to be followed by the congregations themselves. The buildings of planks and bricks and mortar remained, but the living stones were removed. Churches once dedicated to the glory of God for the blessing of men stood bleak, cold, dead—fitting monuments to a departed glory. In one city 23 churches of one denomination alone moved out of the inner city. In another large city 54 churches of all denominations had, within 15 years, closed their doors and moved to the suburbs.

The shift of congregations from the inner city to the outlying districts and the suburbs did not always follow the same time schedule. Sometimes it happened at the first appearance of a Negro family in the community. Sometimes the shift was slower in pace. The congregation could accept a compromise solution—two parishes, one congregation. Some, desiring to keep the ship on an even keel, followed the counsel of "waiting to see what the Lord wanted them to do"—and in the end abandoned the community because of dwindling membership.

One type of response to the new situation was that of a church of affluent members located on a social island not far from the inner city. Beyond the first three or four blocks of the church in either direction, Southern Appalachian mountain folk and Negroes were living. When confronted with their responsibility and as a gesture of seeming Christian concern, the congregation gave permission for conducting a vacation Bible school for the Negro and mountain children. The permission was given with the explicit understanding that there was to be no immediate follow-up. The children and their parents were not to be invited to Sunday school and church. A further gesture was made: after 4 years the congregation would move out of its facilities—estimated at a replacement value of more than a million dollars. The church property would be given over to the denomination's board for missions to establish a mission for the newcomers of the community. There was "heresy" involved in the planned procedure. The church edifice and the other buildings had been dedicated to God for His use. Now they were going to take God's prerogative by giving away what belonged to Him. Their "magnanimity" became even more obvious: others were now to undertake the work which by the blessing of God had fallen to them.

STATISTICS A DETERMINING FACTOR

Dollars and numbers, when correctly used in the function of the church, are for the glory of God. Dollars: "Take my silver and my gold, not a mite would I withhold"; numbers: "All the ends of the earth shall remember and turn to the Lord, and all the families of the nations shall worship before Him" (Ps. 22:27). The people into whose hands the direct development of the church as an institution has been given—the officers of the local congregation and the pastor and, on the higher level, the hierarchy, or district or national church officials—are very often tempted to make dollars and numbers the final criteria in the development of the institution. But when *race* becomes an element in the acceptance or rejection of people, the members of the congregations make race a criterion for membership. It is they, then, who reject God by rejecting people. This rejection is expressed overtly or subtly, but in both cases cuttingly, in the form of threats of withholding financial support from the work of the church or of quitting the church.

When dollars and numbers become the all-pervading criteria for the church's success, something very serious has happened to the institution: people have been rejected, and with the rejection of people goes the rejection of God (see 1 John 4:20). Since the church as an institution exists for the promulgation of the knowledge of God and for His acceptance, the deed or the attitude by which He is rejected makes the institution and all whom it represents grossly hypocritical and worthy of rejection.

A thoroughgoing study of the church in racial crisis was made by two social psychologists of Harvard University. The crisis was the Little Rock incident when Governor Orval Faubus called out the state militia to keep nine Negro children from entering Central

High School. According to this study, fear caused the clergymen of Little Rock not to speak and act according to their convictions. It was the fear of the loss of financial support for the church's budget and fear of the loss of members which would in turn help to deplete the church's treasury and cause the church and the minister to lose the success image. Under the pressure of racial prejudice the ministers succumbed. The role of the expedient administrator robbed the minister of the role of God's prophet.

The Little Rock ministers were no exception to the rule. The fear of the loss of financial support and the concomitant loss of members is a major factor that keeps the church from taking its God-intended place of leadership in the civil-rights movement and the struggle against injustice.

The Clergy

To understand where the church was in the thirties when race became a major issue, one must understand the relationship between clergymen, Negro and white. This interracial clergy relationship was largely structured by the denominational theological preparatory schools and seminaries. The overwhelming number of Negro clergy who received any theological training at all received it in Negro schools. Theological training, for all practical purposes, was on a segregated basis. The result was that the clergy, both Negro and white, were prepared for segregation in the church and thus ill-prepared for the challenge that would confront them in coming decades when race relations would become one of the greatest challenges of the 20th century.

When theological training is given in deliberate segregation, the very purpose of theology is thwarted. Rather than uniting, which is the intent of the Gospel, such segregation separates those who in their calling are to become the heralds of a God-given unity. The performance of the Negro clergyman whose theological training was received in isolation from his white fellow clergymen, and therefore also from the mainstream of the life of his church denomination, can (and often has) become a caricature of the real thing. The Negro minister tries to be what his practical training has kept him from being—a part of the church's tradition. "There is something thrilling about the discovery of a salient theological heritage," [8] which historical circumstances have quite generally denied the Negro clergy.

When a certain kind of skin color becomes a prerequisite for the Christian ministry, then race is made to be a virtue or a vice. In either case the doctrine of the Christian ministry is vitiated, and God's good creation is denied.

There were certain notable exceptions to the rule of segregation within the local congregation. Here and there, especially in the North, and usually where the number of Negroes in the community was small, several Negroes or even several Negro families could find their way into membership in a congregation of white constituency. But the clergy caste system was most rigid; in fact, it was so well established that from the least to the greatest in the church it was never even discussed. Whether episcopal or congregational polity was followed in the calling and placement of clergy to congregations, this was the unquestioned law: Negro clergymen were always called or assigned to Negro congregations.

The clergy caste system was a disgrace to the church. It placed a stamp of inferiority not only upon the Negro clergy but also upon those to whom they were to minister. The system could be considered a violation of creation in that it was also based on the assumption that a Negro clergyman could not serve the best interests of white Christians. Perhaps because of the loss to the church of the Negro clergy potential, the church was compelled to move into a new era of history, the greatest challenge of all times, in an advanced state of spiritual anemia.

3

Catalytic Agents

> Fear wist not to evade as Love wist to pursue.
>
> Francis Thompson[1]

Because of the rapid progress made in the 19th and 20th centuries by the physical sciences—in industrialization, mechanization, automation, and urbanization—the whole face of the earth is changing fast. All the peoples of the earth are now, in a sense, next-door neighbors; they see each other's dirty linen and can easily help to make it appear dirtier than it is. Narrowing this concept down to the United States and its centuries-old race problem, it is easy to see that the "good old days" of white supremacy and racial segregation are now being challenged as never before.

Education with a Purpose

Negroes learned the meaning of the word "freedom" when they were compelled to fight for it to help "save the world for democracy." But when they returned home and were denied the very essentials of our boasted democracy, they were disillusioned. If they were willing to fight for freedom in foreign lands, with machine guns and grenades in their hands, it must be anticipated that when the opportunity presented itself they would fight for freedom at home where it can be practiced; and the battle is now going on.

The battle is being waged on an ever-widening front and with many weapons: by the ballot where it is available; and by protest and every manner of legitimate action to force the reactionaries to know that Negroes will not give up the struggle until the shackles of unjust racial discrimination forged on many anvils of segregation are broken, for themselves and for their children, and the bonds of a hypocritical "separate but equal" are removed from the minds of their oppressors so that they too can be free.

The first and second generation of sons and daughters of those Negroes who fought for the freedom of us all in two world wars are now coming out of high school and college. They have heard the stories of their fathers' experience, when they fought in foreign lands for our freedom and were denied it as they returned to their homeland. With these stories fixed indelibly in their minds and recalled by their own day-by-day experiences with segregation, these sons and daughters of our Negro veterans are not only not satisfied with the type of "freedom" accorded their parents and grandparents; it must be expected that they will want to do for themselves at home what their fathers did for all of us abroad—fight for freedom. And education is a means toward that freedom.

Many of our white high school and college students have enjoyed the advantages of being white; they have lived in middle-class communities and homes with all the comforts and luxuries that the technological skills of our age could produce and the natural resources of the nations of the earth could supply. Not having tasted want, deprivation, and discrimination themselves, they have not been able to appreciate the depth of suffering caused by poverty, disease, hunger, and exploitation under which more than half of the peoples of the earth are now living. Some of our white youths have been exposed to the statistics which tell the story of suffering humanity in Asia, Africa, and Latin America, but the statistics remain to them theoretical abstractions because neither they nor their parents have experienced such suffering themselves.

Many of the Negro young people now coming out of high school and college see themselves as brothers and sisters of the "have-nots" of the world, not merely because the have-nots are by and large people of darker complexion, but because Negroes themselves, having lived in the land of greatest plenty, have been denied their share of that plenty. Now that the lot of the unfortunate colored peoples of the world is being made known and a great world-engulfing struggle is going on to change their lot, it is not difficult to understand the plausibility of our Negro youth identifying themselves with the colored peoples of the world, the have-nots, and also with the revolutionary process intended to change the social order of our times.

Many of our white college students seem to have no higher goal in gaining an education than to secure for themselves and their families a higher standard of living and as much economic security as possible; and many co-eds seem bent on but two things: making passing grades and gaining husbands who will secure for them what the male students are intent upon securing. Because of their background, their present need for complete political emancipation, and their personal identification with the worldwide struggle for freedom and its hoped-for blessings, our Negro students are at a distinct advantage when compared with their white contemporaries. At least a large percentage of the most knowledgeable among our Negro students have a vision and feeling of destiny; the world must change, is going to change, and is even now in the process of change, and they feel themselves in the heart of it and indeed a part of it.

Improved Economic Standards

In an environment of revolutionary change involving many elements, of which educational opportunities are a major factor contributing to the development of the Negro potential, the improvement of the economic standard of Negroes is another element. It acts as a catalytic agent urging them to work toward and to demand their occupying a rightful place in our society as peers among peers of first-class citizens.

At a church convention in the middle thirties the question of integrating congregations of Negro constituency into the organic structure of the church denomination was discussed. At the close of the convention a high-ranking church official in private conversation said, "Give the Negro a little, and he will soon want everything." Although this statement must be rejected in the context in which it was made, there is an element of truth in it. There is a divinely bestowed instinct in man—if not hindered by certain societal conditions or self-imposed inhibitions—that will demand for himself that degree of liberty that guarantees him justice and full equality. When one impediment to his freedom has been removed—for example, illiteracy—he will be able to move faster toward the removal of other impediments; and poverty, or a low economic standard, is another such hindrance.

For generations Negroes have been our hewers of wood and drawers of water. They have built our roads and dug our ditches. They have fought valiantly in our wars and have turned a deaf ear to political enemies who would destroy us. Negroes have given unswerving allegiance to our nation. And yet, by design or indifference we have until now allowed them to go unrewarded. They have been and are, as a group, at or near the bottom of the economic totem pole. "The income of Negro families and individuals nationally . . . is still little more than one-half that of white families and individuals; and in the South Negro families have an income of less than one-half (46%) that of white families and only one-half the income of their non-Southern counterparts."[2]

The other side of the coin shows that, though Negro economic improvement has not begun to measure up to that of the rest of the nation, Negro economic status has improved. Despite the continuing disparity between the income of both groups, there are today many more Negroes with money than there ever have been in our history. In 1960 three times as many Negroes were employed in income-producing, nonagricultural jobs as in 1940. The number of Negro families with an income between $4,000 and $6,000 tripled from 1945 to 1961, and during the same period of time those with an income of more than $6,000 increased from 4% to 20%.[3]

There is still power in the United States dollar. "The power of the Negro market has meaning in the area of race relations, as a 'new' force underlying efforts on the part of Negroes to eliminate discrimination and segregation and obtain better employment in retail trade, industry, and finance."[4] These gains act as spurs that are driving the Negro community unrelentingly to seek equality of opportunity in every area of social life.

Although many of us may be inclined to interpret the patriotic oratory of Fourth of July speakers as clichés that might well be omitted, Negroes, because of the gains made, might hear them and take hope.

Preachment of Democracy

At times the humble listener in the pew, who takes to heart the message of the forgiveness of sins delivered from the pulpit, teaches the preacher the real meaning of his words by applying the message to his own life and that of others. In like manner our Negro citizens have heard our patriotic oratory. Is it not possible that they are now going to teach us how our words are to be applied to practical life situations in the second half of this century?

There has been much preaching in our land about liberty, freedom, democracy, the ballot, the rights of the individual, etc. These words are on the lips of our politicians; they are the meat of their oratory and the substance of textbooks. These words are dinned into the ears of the people of the uncommitted nations and, when we can get through to them, to the people behind the iron and bamboo curtains: the antidote for communism, Castroism, and tyrannical dictatorships of every type and stripe. The politician who lives in a white Northern suburban community, who depends on the votes of his white neighbors, and the Southern patriot as well—all use the same terms. We do have a good form of constitutional government, a good heritage expressed in the Declaration of Independence, in the Constitution as a whole, and in many of the amendments to the Constitution. These "self-evident" truths should be repeated, spelled out, and clarified: "This is our heritage; this is the United States of America."

Perhaps it is the lot and the opportunity of our Negro citizens as well as our other racial or ethnic minority groups to help us distinguish between hypocritical mouthings and words of true patriotic fervor intended to further justice and equity here and elsewhere. For when our words, which obviously have the purpose of bespeaking justice and equity, are used as a camouflage to hide injustice and inequity, they become the means of our own condemnation before the bar of world opinion.

While the preachment of democracy will not let the white man's conscience rest until he has fitted the action to the word, it is the privilege of the underprivileged among us by word and deed to prod, to jab, and to wound our national conscience until we at long last begin to be what in our words we say we are. We dare not despise the impatience of our Negro youth; they are rendering the nation a service of which our own sons and daughters are seemingly incapable. For while the world scene is rapidly changing, many of our Negro youth have in their minds and hands the instruments that can help us bring our deeds to where our words are.

Supreme Court Decisions

In 1789 the founding fathers of our nation declared the Supreme Court to be the final arbiter of the Constitution; and it has been that ever since. Ralph McGill, editor of the Atlanta *Constitution,* said that the Constitution is what the Supreme Court says it is. Some might consider this statement somewhat hyperbolic. There is substance to it, nevertheless; at least that seems to be the case if one compares, for example, the Dred Scott decision of 1857 and the Plessy-Ferguson decision of 1896 with many decisions of the Court handed down since 1938. Since that time, with but few exceptions, the Supreme Court has made decision after decision placing the Constitution on the side of the abolition of segregation and the establishment of the civil rights of the individual citizen.

The 1948 decision (Shelley v. Kraemer) spoke especially to the people outside the South in areas into which Negroes had moved and were to continue to move. Because of the stereotypes employed by many (which spread like wildfire wherever Negroes had moved in considerable numbers or where it was feared they would move), some white people, out of fear and for what they considered the protection of their property, had banded together in neighborhood improvement associations. The object of these associations, expressed in some instances in unmistakable language and in others more subtly, was to keep Negroes and others of a racial or ethnic background different from that of the dominant white group from buying, renting, building, or leasing property in the geographic confines of the specific neighborhood involved. The members of these associations signed documents to that effect.

The 1948 decision of the Supreme Court, while not declaring such neighborhood restrictive covenants unconstitutional, stated that they are unenforceable in courts of law and therefore not legally binding on those signing them. The decision brought freedom to thousands of white property owners. They could now sell to whom they chose regardless of the covenant into which they had entered—in some instances to "protect" themselves, in others to save face with their neighbors.

Although other methods were found to "safeguard" property and pocketbooks, the Federal Government had spoken through its judicial branch; even a schoolboy could now know who had the right to move his family into a decent home in a decent community, uninhibited by prejudicial discrimination. The Supreme Court, often accused of being tinged with red, had in reality gained a moral and propaganda victory over the Kremlin. But the decision that helped to turn the tide and place the Supreme Court, the Federal Government, and the whole nation against segregation as such was the Brown v. Board of Education decision of May 17, 1954.

Other decisions of the Court handed down since the beginning of the thirties attacked the unequal aspect of certain types of segregation and called for the elimination of segregation in specific instances because the system in question did not measure up to the Plessy-Ferguson requirements of "separate *but equal.*" The 1954 decision was radically different. It was in effect a rejection of legalized segregation as such.

It was now abundantly clear that the Supreme Court had reversed itself. The Court of 1954 had now torn down the foundation for legalized segregation built by the Court of 1896, upon which American society, especially in the South, had been building ever since. Both sides were in agreement on this point. Those working for the elimination of segregation wherever the law has jurisdiction were jubilant; to many of them it was a new VE and VJ Day combined—a new emancipation proclamation. The fetters of slavery had been broken, and now those of segregation were to fall, too. It was Black Monday, however, for those on the other side of the fence. They knew exactly what it meant to their "way of life" called segregation: if and when the decision would be carried out, the whole wall of segregation would crumble. Both parties were right.

The decision of May 17, 1954, covered several cases that had been brought before the Court by the National Association for the Advancement of Colored People. Although there were good reasons for quick action, the Court had not acted quickly. It was only after about 2 years had passed that the Court spoke. And finally, after the decision was made public, another year passed before the Court handed down its "with all deliberate speed" decision in which it told the States involved the specific manner in which the desegregation process was to take place.

In the decision itself the Court interpreted the Constitution. It referred neither to the violent opposition that was evidently to follow nor to the dilemma in which our nation stood because of changing conditions in the world. It would nevertheless be wrong to infer that the Court was unaware of these facts or unmindful of them. The Court, too, had come to the crossroads. It was within the power of the Court to affirm the Plessy-Ferguson decision to satisfy the segregationists. In doing so, however, it would have defied world opinion and jeopardized our already dubious status among the nations. It was also within the power of the Court to forsake the philosophy of "separate but equal" and run the risk of incurring the wrath of the segregationists. In that event it would have spoken to our times by recognizing the equality of all citizens before the law and thus opening the way toward gaining or regaining the confidence of two thirds of the world's population—the so-called colored peoples of the world. The die was cast; the Court chose the latter.[5]

The effect of the decision was what might have been anticipated. The border states—Missouri, Kentucky, West Virginia, and Maryland—soon began to conform. The South slowly introduced token integration. The Deep South conformed not at all.

By Executive Order

Tokenism in the South and nonconformity in the Deep South continued until measures more drastic than a Supreme Court decision were taken. It was only after the executive branch of the Federal Government began to show its hand, using its police power, that the patterns of tokenism and nonconformity began to weaken. A step that was drastic but nevertheless imperative was taken by President Eisenhower in 1957, the first of its kind since Federal troops were withdrawn from the South at the end of Reconstruction. When the governor of Arkansas defied the Supreme Court and the Federal Government by sending state troopers to Little Rock to keep nine Negro children from enrolling in Central High School, the President sent U. S. airborne troops to see to it that the order of the Court would be obeyed. When Governor Ross Barnett of Mississippi refused the admittance of James Meredith to the university of that state—thus refusing to conform to the mandate of the Supreme Court and giving a bold example of anarchy—President John F. Kennedy first dispatched Federal marshals to Oxford and soon thereafter U. S. troops. A similarly necessary use of police power took place to enforce the Court's order to desegregate the University of Alabama, Tuscaloosa. Governor George Wallace, in a childish, theatrical gesture, stood in the doorway of the university, symbolizing his rebellion against Federal authority and thus compelling the Attorney General to use the police power of the Federal Government to enforce the law.[6]

A Reluctant Partner—the Congress

In 1948 the race issue began to be a major bone of contention at national political conventions. The two parties began vying with each other to build the strongest possible civil rights plank into their platforms. In doing so, however, they were jeopardizing their chances of gaining the Southern vote, which phenomenon in turn called for all the astuteness at their command to nominate candidates that would as much as possible be acceptable to the voters both north and south of the Mason-Dixon line. But with the plank carefully selected and nailed firmly into the platform and with the candidates nominated and elected, virtually nothing of consequence resulted in the way of enactment of civil rights legislation, neither after the 1948 election nor after the 1952 election.

Southern senators were a comparatively small minority in the Senate—almost all of them members of the Democratic Party. But Democratic senators from the North, with few exceptions, were committed to the passage of civil rights legislation. Some Republican senators were in need of the assistance of some of their Southern Democratic colleagues to effect certain legislation that their Northern constituents wanted. The result? Southern Democrats and the Northern Republicans in question formed a coalition—something not altogether uncommon in the halls of Congress—to thwart the enactment of any civil rights legislation; the Southerners did the talking while their Northern Republican coalitionists assisted in the voting.

The threat of filibuster has long been a potent weapon in the hands of Southern senators to thwart effective civil rights legislation. From the time that civil rights became a major political issue until 1957 the filibuster was not only a threat; it was in fact used with complete success.

A breakthrough finally came in 1957. A civil rights bill was introduced. Because of Southern opposition and the threat of another long-drawn-out filibuster, the bill was watered down by amendment after amendment to a shadowy vestige and was adopted only after many days of filibustering. It was like a little spray of water coming out of a tiny crack in the dam that was holding back the full flow of the waters of racial justice and equity. That was the weak instrument placed into the hands of the Federal administration, the office of the Attorney General, and the courts of the land to cope with the many-faceted problems of the race issue, which was daily growing more serious. The Civil Rights Act of 1957 called for the establishment of a Federal Civil Rights Commission. But the commission was hamstrung from the outset by a lack of freedom of action.

In the meantime civil rights demonstrations were increasing in number and intensity. By 1963 they had spread to the North and West. In many places, in spite of the wise leadership and guidance of responsible civil rights organizations, some of the demonstrations began to border on the violent; rather, less responsible persons either tried to attach themselves to the orderly demonstrations or began their own not too nonviolent ones.

By the spring of 1963, largely due to the determination of responsible individuals and the leadership of many civil rights organizations, the cancerous disease of racism that had been gnawing at the vitals of our nation for centuries had now become known to us and to the world at large. It was imperative that the Government have a further legal instrument to cope effectively with the problem. In the late spring of 1963, after consulting with a cross section of leaders in many fields—religion, industry, labor, education, etc.—President Kennedy presented a bill to the Congress that was praised by a large segment of the advocates of civil rights.

After the proposed bill came into the hands of the House of Representatives' Rules Committee, it was strengthened by a number of amendments. However, the chairman of the committee, Congressman Howard Smith of Virginia, kept the bill from coming onto the floor of the House as long as he possibly could. Civil rights leaders became skeptical as to the purpose of the bill, thinking it was so all-embracing that Southern opposition would be so intense that it would never be passed by the House. But to the surprise of many, with the help of the minority leader, Charles A. Halleck, the bill—H. R. 7152—was passed.

Informed persons anticipated that the real battle was still to be fought—in the Senate, where many civil rights bills had met their Waterloo. A challenge was now before the Senate the like of which had seldom confronted it. The Southerners' performance was true to their traditional pattern: they opposed the bill. They filibustered for 87 days. But for one or more reasons which may not be altogether clear at this juncture in history, the Southern bloc did not have the support of their Northern coalitionists. Although the Senate minority leader, Everett Dirksen, worked for and obtained several modifications of the bill, he did not oppose it. And what is more, he worked closely with the majority whip, Senator Hubert Humphrey, for the passage of the bill. Senator Dirksen persuaded the majority of the Republican coalitionists—those who needed such persuasion—first to vote for cloture and then for the bill itself. And so the bill was passed in the Senate. There were only several minor skirmishes after the bill was returned to the House of Representatives before it was ratified; with the signature of President Johnson it was enacted into law on July 2, 1964.

This law made possible effective action on the part of the executive branch of the Federal Government to step in and, with police power if necessary, to insure a much wider degree of justice and the exercise by all citizens of the civil rights already guaranteed them by the Constitution.

Racists, Rightists, the Backlash—a Coalition

The battle of Armageddon is not over. It has only begun. A hornet's nest of stinging opposition has been stirred up, and all the hornets have not lost their sting nor their determination to sting again and again until their nest is no longer threatened by those who have stirred it. Things may worsen before they get much better. Symptoms of such a worsening process were evident when the civil rights bill was being debated in Congress and almost shockingly manifest immediately after it was enacted into law; there were riots in several of our Northern cities.

The law is intended to make justice a reality and liberty a blessing for all citizens regardless of race or ethnic distinction. Many have been tasting the good fruits of justice and liberty for years but have been ignorant of the fact—or ignoring it—that other human beings have been denied these basic human needs. Some of those thus privileged may have two ingrown difficulties to overcome—pride and guilt—before they can become fully adjusted to the new law and accept it. They may have to lay aside the pride that is built upon a theory of racial superiority. They may also have to find a different response to a guilt complex that has used race as a scapegoat for their guilt. Racial superiority is their boon, their hope, and their salvation. Take it away and you rob them of their ignorance, and their guilt weighs heavily upon them. Some of them, however, have little of this world's goods. If their race pride is removed by making others their equals under the law, they are robbed of their god, and they lose their humanity altogether. It may take them a long time to readjust their thinking so that they will no longer feel the need and the urge to practice racial discrimination. But justice ceases to be justice if, simply because others are not quite ready to accept its application and implementation, it is not applied when needed. Justice postponed is always injustice, despite the fact that its acceptance by some may be slow in coming.

Many racists find communists behind every social action program intended to rid our land of racial segregation and discrimination. The epithet "communist" is used by them to discredit any constructive action taken by governmental authorities—the United States Supreme Court not excluded—or by civic-minded groups or individuals who work for racial justice. The extreme right-wing groups too, such as the John Birch Society, have as their objective the elimination of communism; they and the racial segregationists become not-too-strange bedfellows.

These right-wing groups have been called the radical right. They may be characterized as opposing change, as trying tenaciously to cling to the past, as wanting to solve modern problems with the same methods and techniques used by our agrarian forebears when the complexities of a modern nuclear age were unknown and undreamed of. To many of them there is a simple solution to all the problems of today's society: to them communism is the one great evil of modern times, and therefore all of society's problems must be seen from that perspective; get rid of communism, and the good old days of our grandparents will be with us again.

> What the right wing is fighting, in the shadow of Communism, is essentially "modernity"—that complex of attitudes that might be defined most simply as the belief in rational assessment, rather than established custom, for the evaluation of social change—and what it seeks to defend is its fading dominance, exercised once through the institution of small-town America, over the control of social change.[7]

Any other approach is suspect, and its advocates come under suspicion: they are either communists, communist dupes, or they play into the hands of the communists.

Some rightists, as do many racists, use fundamentalistic religious doctrines to bolster their arguments to give them an aura of authority. This right-wing stronghold is largely in fundamentalist territory. "Regionally, its greatest political concentration is in the South and in the Southwest, and in California." [8] According to the same author, "the fundamentalist 'regions' have risen to new wealth in the last 15 years or so. The industrialization of the South and the Southwest, the boom in real estate, the gushing wealth of oil in Texas and Oklahoma have transformed the fundamentalist churches and the Southern Baptist movement into a middle-class and upper-middle-class group. Small wonder that, possessing this new wealth, the fundamentalist groups have discovered the iniquity of the income tax.

"The social ideas of fundamentalism are quite traditional—a return to the 'simple' virtues of individual initiative and self-reliance. In political terms, this means dismantling much of the social-security program, eliminating the income tax, reducing the role of the federal government in economic life, and giving back to the states and local government the major responsibilities for welfare, labor, and similar legislation." [9]

Those of the radical right join forces with the segregationists, but not necessarily because they want segregation maintained. They make common cause with the segregationists because an upset in race relations brought about by social action, civil rights demonstrations, and Federal intervention on the side of Negroes will, in their opinion, bring that type of confusion into our land that will give the communists in our midst the opportunity they are looking for to overthrow our government and to bring about communist control, possibly centered in Moscow. The advocates of civil rights therefore are attacked by the radical right because their activities are thought to be part of the modern "socialistic" activities of the Federal Government: the United Nations, big government, the income tax, the nuclear test ban treaty, the elimination of states' rights, civil rights, and a host of other items lumped together as Kremlin-contrived plans for our subversion.

"What is uniquely disturbing about the emergence of the radical right of the 1960s is the support it has been able to find among traditional community leaders who have themselves become conditioned, through an *indiscriminate anti-Communism that equates any form of liberalism with Communism, to judge as respectable a movement which, if successful, can only end the liberties they profess to cherish.*" [10]

Another element is emerging in American society and becoming more visible and vocal since the beginning of the civil rights demonstrations and especially since the 1964 civil rights bill was enacted into law. This element was with us before, it must be stressed, but its existence has now come out into the open. A good aspect of this development is that its presence in our midst is now known by those who are capable of discerning the facts. This element in our society, primarily white citizens of the North and West, is found among those who for a long time have deplored the discrimination practiced against Negroes in the South. But now that action is being taken to eliminate these deplorable discriminations—incidentally also those outside the South, in our big cities, and also the subtler ones in the many suburbs surrounding the big cities—these otherwise good people are reacting unfavorably toward the civil rights cause in general and the Civil Rights Act in particular.

This reaction became evident when in 1964 Governor Wallace of Alabama campaigned in the Democratic primary as a candidate for President of the United States. In two Northern states, Wisconsin and Indiana, he secured 34 and 29.8 percent respectively of the Democratic vote, and in Maryland 42.7 percent. There are other evidences of a sizable white backlash, as this element of our population has been called. A fair-housing ordinance was enacted in racially rather liberal Berkeley, Calif., only to be subjected 6 months later to a referendum; the act was rescinded. In Detroit a fair-housing ordinance was defeated, and thousands of signatures were secured calling for a referendum which would limit the enforcement power of the new state constitution to bar discrimination in housing.

The Rumford Act was intended to eliminate racial and ethnic discrimination in housing in the State of California. At the time of the 1964 election, Proposition 14 was voted on by the citizens of California. It was promulgated by powerful real estate organizations of that state. The purpose of Proposition 14 was to nullify the Rumford Act and make it possible for realtors to discriminate at will against racial or ethnic groups. Similar activities intended to place restrictions on civil rights sought by civil rights groups and guaranteed by the Civil Rights Act have been undertaken in other states and cities.

These three groups—the racists, the rightists, and the white backlash—all opposed to civil rights in one form or another, in varying degrees and for different reasons found a banner under which they could march together to obtain a more or less common objective. That banner was woven out of the words and deeds of the 1964 Republican candidate for the presidency of the United States. That this statement is true may be denied by him and many of his supporters. That his words and deeds—his senatorial voting record—were thus understood by the members of these three groups is clearly evident. The dramatic symbol of the segregationist response to the words and deeds of the candidate was Strom Thurmond—one of the most outspoken enemies of civil rights legislation—who bolted the Democratic Party in the midst of the campaign. A symbol of the acceptance of the radical right was the screaming ovation of the Birchites, who somehow filled many balcony seats at the Cow Palace, when in his acceptance speech the candidate said, "Extremism in the cause of liberty is no vice." The identification of the white backlash with the same candidate and, under his banner, also with the segregationists and the radical right was symbolized in the warm reception he received in many places where the white backlash was in evidence—Hammond, Ind., for example, a city which Governor Wallace carried in the Democratic primary.

The candidate under whose banner these three segments of our society—the segregationists, the radical right, and the backlash—found common allegiance was overwhelmingly defeated. But from the perspective of this chapter, his defeat was not necessarily decisive and for the same reason perhaps not all-important. What must be a matter of concern to all who want justice and equity to prevail is that these three dissident groups, each one in itself a somewhat small minority, not only exist but have found a rallying point in one of the two major political parties of our two-party system. The leadership of the party that was so ignominiously defeated and the course it will take may not be fully determined for some time. If, however, the coalition of the three groups continues, the danger is that the party with which they have identified themselves will become a white party, with all the possibilities of an ongoing and intensified racial issue that could disrupt national solidarity, undermine our economy, disillusion our allies and the entire free world, and give our enemies open season to capitalize on one of our primary internal weaknesses.

In all this political ferment our Negro citizens, together with other racial and ethnic minority groups, are involved. But they are not pawns merely to be retained or sacrificed in the interest of sound political strategy for the good of the rest of the nation; nor are they and their interests to be sacrificed to satisfy the selfish ambitions of people who refuse to accept change. They are people whose voices will be heard and whose actions will in a large measure determine the end result of the revolutionary process which is moving faster day by day toward a totally different tomorrow which no one can fully foresee.

Is Time Running Out?

The Marcus Garvey movement of the years immediately following World War I had as its purpose moving Negro Americans to a country to be set aside for them in Africa. Long denied full citizenship in this land, many Negroes were attracted to the movement. The movement itself, though, was but the surface rumbling of a far deeper discontent with the status of our entire Negro citizenry, a discontent which was growing and in the expression of which many Negroes were becoming more articulate.

Originating in the early thirties, a new movement developed which in many ways is far more serious than the Marcus Garvey movement. It is the political-religious cult of the Black Muslims. Their present leader, Elijah Muhammad, claims direct revelation from Allah: he, Elijah Muhammad, is the prophet of Allah; all nonwhites are the children of Allah; all whites are the children of the devil; Elijah Muhammad has been sent by Allah to declare to the "black people" of the United States, the "so-called Negroes," that the hour of their delivery has come; all nonwhite people of the earth are to come into their glory as the children of Allah, while the children of the devil, the whites, are to be destroyed; a first step in the march toward freedom on the part of the "blacks" in the United States is the establishment of a separate state or states where they will be free from the domination of their former masters.

The exact number of Black Muslims is not known, but it is thought by some to be between 100,000 and 200,000 at this writing (1967). The great majority of those who have become members of the cult are recent emigrants from the rural South who are now living in the blighted areas of our metropolitan centers in the North. In the main they are the disillusioned, illiterate, or semi-illiterate. The Black Muslims have found a great harvest field among the Negroes in our big city and county jails.

"Black Power!" Is it a concept or a slogan? Is it something intended to bring the legitimate rights of Negroes, long denied them, to the attention of those who sit in the seats of power? It is claimed by some that Black Power can be a simple expression of the dignity of the manhood of those whose faces are not white, to inspire them to stand tall and strong in their created dignity, to seek the legitimate redress long overdue for grievances, and to give notice to those who form the power structure in the land that justice and equity must be enthroned or chaos and destruction will result, and that right soon.

In some places Black Power has been used to inflame the passions of youth to lay aside reason, caution, and wholesome restraint. Where it has been used, in Tampa, Montgomery, Atlanta, Cincinnati, Dayton (Ohio), Newark (N. J.), and other places, it has caused wanton destruction of property and cruel shedding of blood.

What Black Power is and what its effects are will probably not be fully known and understood until it can be perceived in the perspective of objective historical research.

Such movements have come and gone; and both the nation and the church are still here and perhaps the stronger because of them. The most serious aspect of these movements, though, is that the complaints against the Christian church, as well as American society (within which the church moves), are largely true. Eradication of the movement without the removal of the cause of these just complaints will but add fuel to the fire that has already taken on the proportions of a conflagration.

There are ominous signs of unrest, especially among the youth of our underprivileged nonwhite minorities, primarily Negroes and Puerto Ricans. And there have been destructive riots in many metropolitan centers as well as in smaller communities. Unless the root cause—racial and ethnic discrimination and a grossly apathetic indifference toward the just complaints of the underprivileged—is eliminated, riots will happen again and again, with ever greater danger to many more communities and to the nation as a whole.

In the keynote address delivered at the Republican National Convention July 15, 1964, an ex-president of the United States referred to riots that had taken place only a few days before. He gave little evidence of a sympathetic understanding of the root social, economic, and political causes of such riots. Said he: "Let us not be guilty of maudlin sympathy for the criminal, who, roaming the streets with switchblade, knife and illegal firearms seeking a helpless prey, suddenly becomes, upon apprehension, a poor, underprivileged person who counts upon the compassion of our society and the laxness of or weakness of too many courts to forgive his offense. . . . I submit it is necessary that our substance and our political support help our Governors, our Mayors, and the organizations operating under them, to keep the peace and to maintain order." [11] The applause evoked by the statement was all but uproarious. The statement and the applause were evidence of ignorance of the sociological causes of the riots (and all of us are involved with some degree of guilt) or they were expressions of self-righteous unconcern for the underdog—possibly both. Was the mood of the nation reflected in President Johnson's 1968 State of the Union message and in the reaction of the Congress to that message? When the whole vexing problem of our cities received very little attention commensurate with the need and when the President emphasized the "law and order" approach to the problem, the most vigorous applause of the evening was heard.

As Kenneth B. Clark puts it, there are truths behind the facts. The facts are undeniable. Crime rates, juvenile delinquency, dope addiction, school dropouts, broken homes, and illegitimacy among Negroes are much higher, percentagewise, than among whites. The buildings housing people in the unreconstructed ghetto-slums beggar description. They are often old, dilapidated, filthy, and rat-infested. The hallways in them often stink of urine; garbage and refuse are piled high in the alleys. No knowledgeable, reputable person, Negro or white, will deny these facts. It is the truths behind these facts which, if known and understood, must not only tone down harsh judgment but also turn the accusing finger from the accused to the accuser himself: "You are the man" (2 Sam. 12:7). For what is seen is the cumulative result of three and a half centuries of the bondage of slavery and its equally inhuman successor, segregation. Having been denied the opportunity for an education adequate for our times, those entrapped behind ghetto walls cannot find jobs to sustain themselves and their families; and without education and jobs they cannot secure decent homes, which, even if they could afford them, would nevertheless be denied to them because of race.

The sum total of all of this results in frustration, hopelessness, bitterness, and despair. And when a large segment of the population in our big and crowded cities is, by a calloused and apathetic society, subjected to such intolerable conditions as "the facts" referred to, then look out; trouble is in the wind. If a sick society does not change its ways and the circumstances conditioned by its sickness, there can be but one of two results: the police take over like an army of occupation; or riots, riots, and more riots will break out until our cities will lie in shambles, with our economy wrecked and the nation destroyed.

Is the Biblical dictum being fulfilled—"Whatever a man sows, that he will also reap" (Gal. 6:7)? Basically the problem is theological. What does the church have to say when addressing itself to the race issue? And what is a relevant theology for the church as it faces and tries to come to grips with the issue?

4

From the Perspective of Creation

O Lord, our Lord, how majestic is Thy name in all the earth!

Psalm 8:1

The Nature of Creation

We must assume from the Genesis account of creation as well as from all that the Scriptures of the Old and New Testaments say about God and man that man is unique in God's creation. God took of Himself, of His own life, and gave it to His creature, man, so that man in truth might be called the son of God. As Andrew Schulze received his life from his parents, so man in the creation received his life from God. This is the way the Genesis account puts it: "God said, 'Let Us make man in Our image, after Our likeness.' . . . So God created man in His own image, in the image of God He created him; male and female He created them. . . . The Lord God formed man of dust from the ground, and breathed into his nostrils the breath of life; and man became a living being"–unique among all that God had made, because man was made in the image of God and made alive by the breath of God.

As a child born of human parents is a member of the family that has its origin from those parents, so man, in whom the life of God is found, is a member of God's family. God is the Father. Man is the son of God. "We are the offspring of God" (Acts 17:29). This thought is basic to the whole understanding of the race issue. The human family is one, and according to God's purpose in creation, the human family is God's family.

As children of the same parents may inherit different traits, one being a brunette, another a blonde, one tall, another not so tall, so it is in the family of mankind. Some have been classified according to their several inherited physical traits as Mongolian, others as Caucasian, still others as Negro. But all are human, members of the human family. And what is more, *all* of the human family are "the offspring of God."

Since man was created by God to be a child of God and for that reason a member of His divine family, there is an intimate relation between man and all else that God created. God has made man to be the master, under Him, of the created world and the entire universe. In the Genesis account this is indicated in the simple story: "'Let Us make man in Our image, after Our likeness; and *let them have dominion* over the fish of the sea, and over the birds of the air, and over the cattle, and over all the earth.' . . . So God created man in His own image. . . . And God said to them, 'Be fruitful and multiply, and fill the earth and *subdue it*'" (Gen. 1:26-28).

This thought is amplified by the psalmist: "Thou hast given him dominion over the works of Thy hands." (Ps. 8:6)

Satellites launched into outer space by man are now orbiting the earth. Human beings have been dispatched in capsules to orbit the earth and to return safely. Space rockets have landed on the moon as a precursor to man's landing there. The moon is now the goal of man. What next? No matter what it may be, it is not beyond man's prerogative. He may dig deep into the earth to exploit its treasures, he may split the atom, he may explore and exploit space. That is his prerogative, perhaps his duty. How rich man is according to God's purpose in creation! When singing the praises of God, the psalmist says concerning God's creature, man: "Thou hast made him little less than God." (Ps. 8:5-8)

Whatever in God's good creation is of value belongs to man, to every man. Evenhanded justice, then, is man's due. It is due every man. Man owes it to his fellowman that he too be recognized as one for whom the creation is intended.

It is "in the nature of things," in the very nature of creation, that all of God's human creatures—the Negro, the Mongolian, the Caucasian, and people of every racial strain—should, as far as man's relationship to man is concerned, have equality of opportunity with every other man. Anything less than that is diabolical injustice. That is what the prophet Micah meant when he wrote: "He has showed you, O man, what is good; and what does the Lord require of you but to do justice . . . ?" (6:8)

Man in the communion of a family relationship with God is intended by the Creator to "enjoy" God and everything that God has created. God's purpose in creation was that man, in communion with his God and under the everlasting rays of His love, enjoying all that God had created and finding God's goodness reflected in creation itself, was to "feel good all over." To have as our goal for all of the human family anything less than that is not only to deny the humanity of some of God's creatures but to sell short the Creator Himself.

Creation's Ultimate Purpose

Man in a happy family relationship with God is not the final purpose of the creation. In this blessed condition man is not another god, nor an addition to the Trinity. God remains the Creator-God, and man (together with all else) remains God's good creation. God alone is the preeminent One. All creation is there to serve the Creator; *God is to be glorified in all things.*

God's faithful people in Old Testament times acknowledged the purpose of creation and fulfilled it as they praised the name of the Creator: "Thine, O Lord, is the greatness and the power and the glory and the victory and the majesty; for all that is in the heavens and in the earth is Thine; Thine is the kingdom, O Lord, and Thou art exalted as Head above all. Both riches and honor come from Thee, and Thou rulest over all. In Thy hand are power and might; and in Thy hand it is to make great and to give strength to all. And now we thank Thee, our God, and praise Thy glorious name." (1 Chron. 29:11-13)

In the Lord's Prayer Christ teaches us to pray for our needs as well as those of others, for spiritual and physical needs, so that all those blessings intended by God in the creation of the world may be realized. But that is not the end. According to some ancient authorities, Christ directs His followers not only to trust in the goodness of God to hear and answer their prayers, but He enjoins them to pray to the glory of God; this is added to the prayer as we have it in the glorious doxology: "For Thine is the kingdom and the power and the glory forever." (Matt. 6:13 KJV)

That is the happy picture. God the Creator is the Father of the human family, to whom He has given divine life; the human family is one in created dignity and one in the privilege of using and enjoying all that God has created; the human race was created in the image of God so that all of creation should be used to the glory and praise of the Creator.

If all that God created, including man, is according to God's purpose in creation to serve but one end, the glory of God, then all of creation must be approached with reverence and in the fear of God. Men doff their hats as they enter a library, and well may they do so, for on its shelves are the records of the wisdom of the ages, a gift of God's goodness. One can understand and perhaps approve of a custom still practiced in the Kremlin in Moscow. Fabulous treasures of art fashioned through many generations by the skillful hands of men and women, many of whom have been dead for centuries, have been deposited behind the Kremlin wall in an ancient building called the Armoury. Before visitors may enter its spacious halls they must slip carpet-bottomed slippers over their street shoes, possibly to serve a double purpose: to be a symbol of reverence and respect and a means of preserving the floors.

But created things and man himself with all his talents and skills are to be approached with respect and reverence because the dignity that is theirs is a reflection of the dignity of the Creator, "for from Him and through Him and to Him are all things" (Rom. 11:36). The two must go together: genuine respect for the dignity of the creature created by God, and the fear of God Himself. As man in his physical state, living in a universe of created things, glorifies the Creator, he must do so in the context of a proper relationship to things created and especially to man created to be a son of God.

God's Plan in Creation Frustrated

Looking about in the world as it really is, one finds conditions quite the opposite from God's purpose in creation. Man is in rebellion against his heavenly Father, the divine Creator. Man has chosen death instead of life. By rejecting the life which God alone could give, man chose to die. Death is now man's lot. "The day that you eat of it you shall die" (Gen. 2:17). "As sin came into the world through one man and death through sin . . . so death spread to all men because all sinned" (Rom. 5:12). In contemplation of man's deadness, the prophet Isaiah says, "In full vigor we are like dead men." (59:10)

By giving up the life with which God had endowed him, man also tore himself loose from his neighbor. The loss of real human brotherhood between man and man is set forth in the story of the slaying of Abel by Cain. (Gen. 4)

Because of the double estrangement of man—first from God and second from his neighbor—the whole creation is now out of kilter. Man, having rejected both God and his neighbor, seeks only his own good and his own glory.

From the dawn of recorded history to this day man has been in constant conflict with his fellowman. This unpleasant and humiliating fact was never more clearly to be seen than it is today: Conflict between the West and the East; between communist Russia and communist China; between the United States and its allies; between management and labor; between whites and nonwhites;

between Christian and Christian: Roman Catholic, Protestant, and Orthodox; and between husband and wife. There have been two fratricidal world wars within the memory of many now living; and every second day we are at the brink of a third world war that threatens the destruction of all life on earth. It is not an altogether happy prospect in which man in his state of rebellion against God finds himself.

Man can examine much of God's good creation. He can distinguish one element from another. He can separate the elements and put them together again. And he can learn to use them. With his finite understanding man can recognize the wisdom and power of God, who still preserves all that He has created, working normally through what are called natural laws to sustain the whole universe according to a divine plan by which all things continue to be and to serve a divine purpose. But man in his state of rebellion against God finds himself to be the one great enigma. He is without purpose, and his whole existence is a living death. His self-centered existence makes it impossible not only to understand who he is and why he is here but also to understand who his fellowman is; nor can he in truth be of lasting help to him. In the final analysis, even in his most loving deeds, done in his most charitable mood, he will only be serving himself. The underlying motive for everything he thinks, says, and does is, "What will I get out of it?"

> By nature we are totally self-centered and our interests take a centripetal direction. We are prone to take up our position at what we feel to be the center of the universe and expect or compel everything to move in toward us.[1]

The life of God given to man in creation is God-centered. Self-centeredness, then, is an existence devoid of the divine life.

> Racial prejudice is an expression of man's sinful self-centeredness. Viewed historically, racial prejudice, in the Christian sense, is not really a new thing but simply the latest and most virulent form of man's ancient urge for self-exaltation. Thus far, the history of antagonistic human relationships, despite the many varieties, has a single, simple, and inclusive definition: it is the story of the periodic substitution of one bias for another; it is the story, not of the correction of prejudice, but of the conversion of prejudice from one object to another; it is the story of a central

and consistent motivation in the will of man, assuming at different times and different places various cloaks and armors and assorted victims. The circles defining the "in-group" and the "out-group" have circumferences that rove and shift, now including and then excluding the same people; but the center of each such circle remains constant, that center being the prideful self-centeredness of the individual. Racial prejudice is merely one of these shifting and recurrent circles.[2]

This self-centeredness of man is attested to by Christian theology and by the clear record of history, not excluding current history. Modern studies in psychology and psychiatry have a tendency to substantiate what Christian doctrine has to say about the self-centeredness of man. Sigmund Freud, who was no Christian, said: "In the undisguised antipathies and aversion which people feel toward strangers with whom they have to do, we recognize the expression of self-love, of narcissism." [3]

Self-Centered Man Defies Laws of God and Man

Man's self-centeredness finds its expression in the amoral man, the man who at least seemingly flouts the law, whether it be the moral law of the Bible or the laws of men. It is in response to an inner urge to preserve his god, self, that we have our gangster, our gang leader, our corrupt politician, and our modern demagogue.

This type of idolatrous self-preservation will move a state governor to call out an army of state troopers to keep nine Negro children from attending a school built and maintained by the funds secured in part through the taxes paid by their parents. The idolatrous nature of man is expressed in the defiance of the law of the land and the explicit direction of a Federal court when the governor of a state, through inflammatory speeches and rebellious remarks, whips up the emotions of semi-illiterate, racially prejudiced whites with the result that the President of the United States is compelled to bring hundreds of U. S. marshals to a state university campus to enrol one Negro student, an ex-GI who wants to complete his education at the university in his home state supported by the taxes of all citizens of that state. Like Pontius Pilate, the governor may try to disclaim the guilt involved in the death of a foreign correspondent and an innocent onlooker from a nearby town. It was not merely the inevitable result of an unfortunate background on the part of the same governor that caused him to continue to defy the Federal Government and the Federal court and which encouraged someone on the lunatic fringe to kill Medgar Evers; the governor was trying to save himself—an expression of his depraved, man-centered human nature.

The same may be said of the governor when, with a flair for the dramatic and with eyes on the possible political advantage accruing from it, he stood in the doorway of the university of his state, thus symbolically keeping the first Negro from entering that school and thereby incidentally disclaiming the oath of obedience to the Constitution of the United States taken at the occasion of his inauguration. The bombing of the church in Birmingham, Ala., on Sept. 15, 1963, which caused the death of four children, and the governor's erratic, anarchical statements and activities are not unrelated. And both are tragic expressions of man's alienation from God and his neighbor, a perversion of God's purpose in creation, and, if properly understood, evidences of man's idolatrous self-centeredness.

It was only a few weeks after the momentous May 17, 1954, Supreme Court decision declaring racial segregation in public schools unconstitutional that Lillian Smith's book *Now Is the Time* was published. In it Miss Smith not only traces the development of the segregation system that has plagued the nation and the church for almost a century, but she links demagoguery and the segregation pattern together, showing that the self-interest of the demagogue is a predominant factor in the origin, development, and continuation of segregation: "The politicians had picked up 'the Negro issue' like a football and were tossing the destiny of millions back and forth in their political games." [4]

In self-seeking duplicity, demagogues elected to the United States Senate often stymie the whole function of the governmental process. After the late President Kennedy had introduced his civil rights program to the Congress, *The Christian Century* said editorially:

> These congressmen, who plan to conduct a filibuster to defeat civil rights legislation, are the same congressmen who denounce Supreme Court decisions in the field of civil rights and who demand that the court leave the making of the nation's laws to the legislative branch of government.

> Insisting on the one hand that Congress has sole responsibility for the making of the nation's laws, on the other hand they use the filibuster to prevent legislation in the most crucial and dangerous area of the nation's life.[5]

The "Good" Self-Centered Man

The other side of man's self-centered idolatry can be expressed in a zeal for the Law, for justice and righteousness, when that zeal has its motivation in a desire to gain the favor of God by keeping the Law and thus exalting the spiritually dead man into a position of God's good man while rejecting God's good life. In the center of the controversy that runs throughout the gospels and the epistles, especially the epistles of St. Paul, is the endeavor of man to justify his godless state by doing good, by keeping the Law, by himself doing "justice and showing mercy," or by "doing the right thing for the wrong reason."

That which was to the religious leaders of Christ's day probably the most exacerbating aspect of His ministry was the company in which He was so often found. First one might think of those whom He chose to be His disciples. They were not selected from the elite of His time; perhaps their allegiance to governmental authority was seriously questioned by many. All of the Twelve, with the exception of Judas Iscariot—and he didn't prove to be a person of highest morals—came from Galilee, which was the hotbed of the Zealots, whose desire to overthrow the existing government by any possible means was not only well known but no doubt also a source of great fear to many. At least four of the Twelve, Peter, Andrew, James, and John, were Galilean fishermen. It is altogether possible that the smell of fish was on their clothes, and the profanity of their kind, which had become a part of their day-by-day conversation, may have been ready to be vocalized at any provocation. It isn't hard to imagine the unprintable words that might have been spoken by them to the Samaritan innkeeper when he refused them and their Master lodging for the night. Altogether justifiable is the omission of such words by the evangelist St. Luke when he reports their having said, "Lord, do You want us to bid fire come down from heaven and consume them?" (Luke 9:54). In view of the age-old hostility between the Israelites and the Samaritans, it is possible that from the recesses of memory of these disciples some dirty word came forth by which they in earlier days had referred to Samaritans. It is possible that the coarse Roman soldiers chuckled when Peter, reverting to his former uncouth way, "began to invoke a curse on himself and to swear" (Mark 14:71). Such were those whom Jesus chose to be His disciples, whom He called His "friends."

Neither was the relationship between Christ and the religious leaders of His day improved when the wider circle of His associates included many of ill repute. Not only did He call Matthew, "sitting at the tax office," saying to him, "Follow Me," but when Matthew obeyed, Jesus went into Matthew's home, "and many tax collectors and sinners came and sat down with Jesus and His disciples." The reaction of His religious adversaries was quick in coming and sharp in its denunciation. They addressed themselves to His disciples in these words: "Why does your teacher eat with tax collectors and sinners?" (Matt. 9:9-11)

On one occasion religious leaders brought a woman to Jesus and told Him that she had been caught in the very act of adultery. They wanted Him to pass judgment on her and implied that, if He did not condemn her, He Himself would be guilty of breaking the Law. This would be incontrovertible evidence that He Himself was unworthy to be heard. But true to His mission, Christ rejected them in their imagined goodness and identified Himself with the woman by saying, "Let him who is without sin among you be the first to throw a stone at her." (John 8:7)

Jesus shocked the law-abiding, self-centered, self-righteous people by keeping company with and accepting those whom they rejected as sinners. He was consistent; His enemies were too. His teachings were in keeping with His life as He accepted sinners; His enemies showed their consistency by rejecting them.

Christ was not another Moses; His teaching was not a teaching of morality; this was exemplified in His dealing with and attitude toward people. Neither the Sermon on the Mount nor the story of the Good Samaritan is the central teaching of Christ. Both are related to that teaching as the Law and the Gospel are related to each other, and still the Law is not the Gospel, neither is the Gospel the Law.

Jesus said of those who claimed to be "disciples of Moses" that they were bypassing the door to heaven, which is Christ, and were trying to get there by another way, that of the Law or their own goodness (John 10:1-10). This must be understood in the context of man's lifelessness when he is without God. That is what Christ told Nicodemus: "Unless one is born anew, he cannot see the kingdom of God." (John 3:3)

Without the "wedding garment" of a new life, the righteousness of Christ, man is rejected by his Creator (Matt. 22:11-14). Jesus told the parable of the Pharisee and the publican to those who "trusted in themselves that they were righteous." They boasted of their goodness as the means of justifying themselves in the sight of God. But Jesus said they "will be humbled" (Luke 18:14). He told His own disciples that without a righteousness greater than that of the moral, law-abiding man, they would "never enter the kingdom of heaven." (Matt. 5:20)

The rich young ruler (Luke 18:18-23) was a man of good moral and ethical conduct who said that he had kept the commandments from his youth. He was sincerely concerned about spiritual matters; he wanted to go to heaven. The young man probably realized that something was still lacking in him. What was that "one thing" that he lacked? That's what he wanted to know from Jesus. Jesus' answer in response to the young man's salutation, "Good Teacher," gives us the key to the problem involved. "Why do you call Me good? No one is good but God alone." The young man, Jesus intimated, needed more than a little more moral goodness. What he needed was God, the source of all goodness. Him he did not have.

From all these examples and many others found in the gospels [6] we learn that Christ did not come into the world to make bad men less bad and good men more good. He rejected any claim of goodness on the part of men, even the best of men who had nothing of which to boast except that they were just "naturally" good people, always getting better by keeping the Law.

Man, separated from God and the life of God, serves self through an idolatrous self-centeredness even when he tries to be good, and then looks to his own goodness as the source of his final security and personal worth. This is the consistent lesson that Christ teaches us by His entire life, especially by the company He kept and the attitude He assumed toward those rejected by society. This is also a consistent emphasis of His teaching and the teaching of the apostles as set forth in the New Testament epistles, especially those of St. Paul. (See Eph. 2:1, 12; 4:18; 1 Tim. 5:6)

In the Letter to the Hebrews we find the author writing about "dead works" (6:1). Like the wax fruit on the table in some households or the wax figures in Madame Tussaud's shop in London, these "dead works" are not the real thing. They may appear to be real and in fact may serve some good purpose in the economy of God for the restoration of creation. But they are without life. God does not accept them. With no life in them, the living God is not glorified by them. St. Paul's opponents taught, or implied in their teaching, that unregenerate man is capable of some moral goodness that merits the attention and acceptance of God. He called such teaching "a different gospel" (Gal. 1:6) and said that those who teach it are perverters of the true Gospel (1:7). He said, "Dead through trespasses and sins." They said, "Dead? Well, maybe, but not altogether so." They implied that there is some innate goodness in man that gives him power to save himself—well, not completely, but through keeping the Law, doing good—perhaps with a little assistance from the Spirit to help make the grade.

The chief opponents of the apostles and of Christ Himself were people who were concerned about goodness, virtue, and justice. This may be a shock to many who sincerely want to lead good moral lives, who want to have their ethical conduct measure up to the highest standards of man and God. If justice and all other virtues are intended by the Creator to be a part of His good creation, then Christ and the apostles as messengers of God must of necessity be teachers and advocates of such virtues. The point to be made in this connection, though, is that the source of virtues that are pleasing to God cannot be found in man who has forsaken God, chosen death, and forfeited the life of God which alone has the power to produce these virtues. Christians can and are obligated to cooperate with persons who do not have the new life that is found in Christ, as many of them do in the current civil rights movement. But the good deeds finally approved and accepted by God are those which are the expression of the new life in Christ. All others, in the final analysis, are an expression of egotistic self-centeredness.

The Love Instinct

Parents love their children, and children love their parents. This is a universal phenomenon. This love is a part of the stuff that helps to make man. He loves instinctively. But this in itself does not set him apart from the rest of creation, from the birds of the air and the beasts of the field. Man cannot live without love. Psychiatrists tell us that the mother's love is as important for the proper growth and maturity of a child as the mother's milk. But the human mother is not essentially different in this respect from the cow, the mare, and other mammals. God has given this "love" instinct to man and to beast. By means of it one generation brings another into the world and thus preserves its kind.

Natural love is in itself a precious gift of God and, as such, something beautiful. Nevertheless, it has its limitations. It cannot bring about a utopian society. While it is a part of the creation and God's continuing creative process, history and present-day human experience prove that natural love can be turned into a powerful weapon of human destruction. This same instinct of love, concentrated in the desire for self-preservation, may unite some people: family with relatives and relatives with more relatives, members of the same ethnic group, and people having the same linguistic or national identity. But while the unity thus established may be for the good of those united, it can become an instrument for the subjugation or destruction of others. Genghis Khan, who became a ruthless conqueror of the medieval world, was not without love, a love for his own people. Prince Otto Eduard Leopold von Bismarck, in the interest of the German people and for the glory of his own German state, by trickery and intrigue purposefully brought about the Franco-Prussian War; and he did it out of love for his own and his own kind.

Because this love instinct is universal, embracing all humankind, it is not unreasonable to suppose that it influenced empire builders from the days of Alexander the Great to the present time as they went out to conquer one province after another, to exploit natural resources, and to secure for their own land or city the wealth and wisdom of others. All of mankind since the Fall has abused the divine gift of love, bringing misery and death upon others.

LOVE, CHAMELEONLIKE

The love of some white Southerners has often embraced Negroes of their acquaintance, their slaves during antebellum days and their servants or employees since then. To picture all white Southerners as negrophobes is caricaturing reality.

Before the Civil War many of the masters and their families learned to know the humanness of their slaves, especially the house slaves. A very cordial relationshp developed and, within certain limitations imposed by Southern white culture, they were regarded and in many ways treated as members of the family. The love that flowed in this instance from the whites to the Negroes was within the solidly structured master-slave relationship. This type of love relationship may still be found among some Southern whites.

> When I was in my teens, I had a memorable conversation with a Southern white man of a generation older than mine. He was one of the kindest men I had ever known. He would do anything for a friend. He was a leader in his church and in the community, and no man in need—friend or stranger, black or white—who ever went to him for help was turned away. But he believed in segregation. He believed in it with a violence that squared with nothing else in his personality. We were discussing the advisability of a federal anti-lynch law, which was at that time a live issue before the country. I was arguing in favor of such a law. My older friend was infuriated that I, a Southern girl, supposedly "well bred," could express such treason. Suddenly in the heat of the argument, he said: "We have to have a good lynching every once in a while to keep the nigger in his place." [7]

People north of the Mason-Dixon line are not devoid of natural love toward their beleaguered brothers and sisters farther south. What many of them write, say, and do in the interest of civil rights cannot be brushed aside as "politically inspired" or the "meddlesome work of outside agitators." The inadequacy of such love becomes evident very often when these high-minded Northerners are forced to put their love for their Southern Negro brothers to the test. Their love then proves to be a love for people that are far away, at least sufficiently removed from them that they themselves are not called upon to demonstrate it through neighborliness.[8] When they are asked to receive Negroes or other nonwhites as next-door neighbors, their altruistic spirit suddenly becomes purely theoretical, without the substance of reality. Then, motivated by pride or fear, their liberality vanishes into thin air, their love turns into or is revealed to be self-love, and all types of rationalization are used to justify their endeavors to keep Negro children out of the schools attended by their sons and daughters or to keep Negro families confined to filthy, crime-ridden, big-city ghettos. "Thou shalt love thy neighbor as thyself" is turned into a law of self-preservation, with property taking precedence over people. The title of C. S. Lewis' book *The Great Divorce*[9] symbolizes man's lostness. In that unique fantasy the author depicts the subtlety of man in his fallen state, even using love at times as a gimmick to preserve the integrity of his sinful, godless, and therefore lifeless existence.

Man in the sinful state in which he is found—and to which both revelation and history attest—is alienated from God and his fellowman. The treasures of creation are now abused by man; he uses them for his own selfish purposes and not to the praise of God or for the well-being of mankind. Even the greatest of all natural virtues is employed by self-centered man to protect and defend his ego. Whether man lives a life of conformity to law or whether he defies the laws of God and man, he is always seeking his own. These facts, humbling as they may be, must be borne in mind if one would understand what is the real nature of the dilemma confronting us in the current race issue.

Is the way of the futilitarian, the fatalist, the stoic, or the epicurean the only possible practical way of life? And beyond that, is there no hope for man in heaven or on earth? There is. It is in a new heaven and a new earth.

5

Life in the Midst of Death

Though he were dead, yet shall he live.
John 11:25 KJV

It was a great day in our nation's history when General Douglas MacArthur, on board the battleship *Missouri* in Tokyo Bay, signed the instrument which brought World War II to a close. Among the now famous words uttered that day, he said, "The problem basically is theological." Equally so, the race problem is theological. When viewed from the perspective of God's purpose in creation, the problem is not solved merely by getting the job done, that is, by extending the borders of justice to include more people. Our primary concern—even when human beings are directly involved as the target of our aim for justice—is not human beings but He in whom we have our being, that is, God. Justice is to be sought for God's sake. Justice is to be established in the world to the glory and praise of God. But the godly alone can praise God in a way acceptable to Him.

According to the Genesis account of the creation of man, two distinct steps were taken by God: man's physical form was first brought into being, and then God gave of His own life. He "breathed into his nostrils the breath of life" (Gen. 2:7), and in doing so He made man in His own image and likeness; He made him "godly." Man was created in the image of God, a son of God, so that he might, as a member of God's family, be found worthy and able to glorify and praise God. But in turning away from God through rebellion against Him, man lost the godly life and made himself incapable of praising Him, that is, of fulfilling his part of God's purpose in creation. It is only through a new life, a new creation in Christ, that man can once again be truly man, the man "after the heart of God," the man who could fit into the scheme of things as planned by the Creator. Justice and equity are good; they are of the "stuff" of creation—like the human, physical anatomy. But if man is without the life that God alone can give, no matter how just he may seem to be in all his dealings with his fellowman, he himself cannot please or glorify God. The organic mechanism of the human body may be there, but it is without spiritual vitality and, for that reason, what man may produce, even the noblest of deeds, is rejected by God.

Dry Bones Become Alive

There is perhaps no clearer Biblical presentation of this whole matter than that of the prophet Ezekiel:

> The hand of the Lord was upon me, and He brought

> me out by the Spirit of the Lord and set me down in the midst of the valley; it was full of bones. And He led me round among them; and behold, there were very many upon the valley; and lo, they were very dry. And He said to me, "Son of man, can these bones live?" And I answered, "O Lord God, Thou knowest." Again He said to me, "Prophesy to these bones, and say to them, O dry bones, hear the word of the Lord. Thus says the Lord God to these bones: Behold, I will cause breath to enter you, and you shall live. And I will lay sinews upon you, and will cause flesh to come upon you, and cover you with skin, and put breath in you, and you shall live; and you shall know that I am the Lord."
>
> So I prophesied as I was commanded; and as I prophesied, there was a noise, and behold, a rattling; and the bones came together, bone to its bone. And as I looked, there were sinews on them, and flesh had come upon them, and skin had covered them; but there was no breath in them. Then He said to me, "Prophesy to the breath, prophesy, son of man, and say to the breath, Thus says the Lord God: Come from the four winds, O breath, and breathe upon these slain, that they may live." So I prophesied as He commanded me, and the breath came into them, and they lived and stood upon their feet, an exceedingly great host. (37:1-10) [1]

What is meant by "the breath" coming "from the four winds" that the slain "may live" is explained in these words: "I will put *My Spirit* within you, and you shall live" (v. 14). While it is true that God is speaking of His dealings with the Israelites, His purpose in revelation is always the same: He is the Creator, and fallen man must be restored so that in and through man God may be glorified.

The Mystery of Heaven and Earth in Unity Again

How the "dry bones" spoken of by the prophet Ezekiel are brought together again and imbued with life, man doesn't know; it is a great and hidden mystery to him. And why? Because in his fallen state he doesn't really know God.

Without knowing God, man may know a great deal about God; and what he knows may even lead him to seek justice and equity for his fellowman, a real concern of this book. But the knowledge of

God that reunites man with God and in a real sense with his fellowman, the knowledge that is needed for that unity which restores God's purpose in creation, is a mystery to man; of himself he cannot know it.

St. Paul in the Epistle to the Ephesians calls this knowledge a mystery. He speaks of "the mystery of His will" (1:9); of "the mystery hidden for ages in God who created all things" (3:9); of how "the mystery was made known to him [St. Paul] by revelation" (3:3). He calls it "the mystery of Christ." (3:4)

To this point an attempt has been made to demonstrate the absence of a life in man which unites him with God and his fellowman. But man, who in himself is without life and hope, may find hope, because he may find life in Christ.

What makes the Christian religion distinctive, different from all other religions, the formal as well as the informal, is not merely a distinctive teaching—although it is that—but a person. That person is Christ.

Christ is the revelation of God to man (John 1:18). God has revealed Himself in Christ so that man might be reunited with God and with his neighbor to the glory of God. When God's appointed time had come, God Himself came into the world. He appeared among human beings as a human being, that is, He became man. God was incarnate in human flesh (John 1:14). In this way He identified Himself with man; He became man's brother. (Heb. 2:11)

Even in his fallen state man is able to know much about God—that He is; that He is just; that He often punishes evil and rewards good. Even without the Incarnation, or the revelation of God in Jesus Christ, man is able to probe into the treasures of wisdom hidden in nature; through study and scientific research much of the riches of God's creation can be uncovered to the wondering gaze of man—a revelation of many things about God the Creator Himself: that He is infinitely wiser than man, that His power is altogether incomprehensible, and even that He is good. When Jesus said that God "makes His sun rise on the evil and on the good, and sends rain on the just and on the unjust" (Matt. 5:45), He was speaking of something that even the evil and the unjust can well know without divine revelation. All they need to do is observe nature. But without the revelation of God in Christ, man cannot know God in His essential being: He cannot know God as *love*.

Christ, the Agape of God

Agape is the Greek word in the New Testament ordinarily translated in the Revised Standard Version by the word love. But the love expressed by the word *agape* is something distinct. It has to do with the very nature of God. It is the *agape* of God that is described in the New Testament as mystery.

Man may know *agape* as a theory, but he has no experiential knowledge of it; in his unregenerate or natural state he has not experienced and cannot experience the *agape* of God. Christ alone can reveal it to man. Christ is God incarnate. The life of God is in Christ, and this *agape* of God is the life of God. "God *is* Love *(agape)*" (1 John 4:8). In the Incarnation a totally new life, God's life, came into the world. It is in essence the same life that man, created in the image of God, lost through sin in the Fall.

The life of Christ as He sojourned among men is described by St. Luke in these words: "He went about doing good" (Acts 10:38). His whole life was a life of love. He healed the sick, gave sight to the blind, fed the hungry, comforted the sorrowing, and brought dead men back to life. He did all of this because of the God-life that was in Him; and the performance of these *agape* deeds was a sign that the kingdom of God had come to men. But the real nature of the *agape* is found in the Cross: the suffering, death, and resurrection of Christ.

By willful disobedience and diabolical rebellion against the God of love, man turned away from God and from the life of God. Man chose death instead of life. If God's purpose in creation, more particularly in the creation of man, was to be restored, death had to be removed; and since death is the inexorable judgment of God upon disobedience to His majestic will, death as divine judgment had to be removed. To accomplish this, God entered into human history as He had never done before: in Christ He became man.

The humanity of Christ was not intended as a dramatic demonstration of humility, nor of divine love at which even the spotless angels of heaven might stand in awe before the God of heaven and earth, enabling them to sing new songs of praise and in some way adding to their "Holy, holy, holy" as they surround the throne of God (Is. 6:1-4). The humanity of Christ was for the purpose of identifying Himself with sinful man in his desperate condition of mortality and in so doing to draw into Himself the judgment of God, which is death, and by dying remove death from man forever.

The death of Christ was not the tragic end of a good life, with its possible example of suffering for the sake of truth and goodness. The redemption of man through the death of Christ was planned by God Himself, and therefore woven into the blueprint of redemption is the divine assurance of victory over death, with life emanating from it.

Heilsgeschichte, or salvation history, with these implications: the promises of God's loving-kindness and tender mercy held out to men throughout the long period of Old Testament history, the fullness-of-time event when God in Christ became man, the whole life of Christ including His going about doing good, His conflict with the Evil One when He was sorely tempted in the wilderness, His betrayal by a friend, His denial by His most articulate supporter, His agony in the garden, His walking the way of sorrows, His dying for mankind on the accursed tree, His cry, "My God, my God, why hast thou forsaken me?" that brought a moment of rejoicing to the demons in hell and a moment of silence in heaven, and His resurrection—all this was the *agape* of God. It was the self-giving, self-sacrificing love of God; it was the very life of God, the mystery revealed in Jesus Christ. It was? No, it is! The life of God is always "is."

The death of Jesus Christ is the gateway to eternal victory over the Evil One, over sin, over death.

The strife *is* o'er, the battle done;
Now is the Victor's triumph won;
Now be the song of praise begun.
Alleluia!

Death's mightiest powers have done their worst,
And Jesus hath His foes dispersed;
Let shouts of praise and joy outburst.
Alleluia!

On the third morn He rose again
Glorious in majesty to reign;
Oh, let us swell the joyful strain!
Alleluia!

The resurrection of Jesus Christ from the dead is man's assurance that death has been vanquished, sin has been atoned for, and God is reconciled to man. He may now return to his rightful, creation-ordained inheritance. There is a place once again for man in the economy of God.

The resurrection of Jesus Christ from the dead is the keystone of the Christian faith. Without it Christianity would be a hoax. St. Paul said, "If Christ has not been raised, your faith is futile. . . . We are of all men most to be pitied." (1 Cor. 15:17, 19)

But how can one know and be sure that Christ lives and that our Christian faith is not in vain? How can others, hearing the message about the living Christ, be brought to a living faith in Him? The living Christ, the Christ in us, is the answer. He Himself is His own proof that He lives.

Christ in Us, Works Through Us

Much of what has been said about Christ must be said about His believing followers: mystery, incarnation, the *agape* life of God. The greatest mystery appearing on the face of the earth since the coming of Christ is found in the Christian believer: The Christ of divine majesty is in the Christian.

When the Christian lives out his Christian life in the great struggle for human justice in the area of civil rights and when he, in the church, brushes aside all racial barriers to accept people without regard for racial, ethnic, or class distinctions, his action is not understood by the world—the world in the church and the world outside the church. While the segregationist will oppose him and the secular humanist applaud him, neither will understand him. Christ Himself was not understood—neither in His person nor in His Messianic calling. Some saw Him healing the sick and feeding the hungry; they wanted to make Him a king. Others looked upon Him as a serious menace to morals and religion; they wanted to destroy Him.

This ignorance concerning Christ, "the Mystery of God," is transferred to the believer in Christ. This is true because Christ is in the Christian believer. God came into human history when Christ was born of the Virgin Mary. That was the holy Incarnation: God in man for the redemption of the world. And now God, in Christ, is found in the Christian believer for the reconciliation of the world. The body of the Christian believer is the temple of Christ, and, through Christ, the temple of God. This type of Christological terminology is found throughout the New Testament, especially in the writings of St. Paul. For example: "Do you not know that *you are God's temple* and that *God's Spirit dwells in you?*" (1 Cor. 3:16); "To them God chose to make known how great among the Gentiles are the riches of the glory of *this mystery, which is Christ in you,* the hope of glory" (Col. 1:27). In His sacerdotal prayer Christ Himself used somewhat similar language: "All Mine are Thine, and Thine are Mine, and I am glorified *in them*" (John 17:10). St. John says: "*He who is in you* is greater than he who is in the world." (1 John 4:4)

With Christ in him the Christian has a new life—the life of Christ, which is the life of the *agape* of God. The *agape* life as lived by Christ and manifested in the cross and the open tomb, and the *agape* life of Christ in the believing Christian have the same ultimate purpose: reconciliation, and its concomitant, unity—the unity of God and man, of heaven and earth, with nothing in God's good creation omitted (Eph. 1:10). In Eph. 3:8-10 St. Paul speaks as though in stage one Jesus Christ was the agent of grace, but now in stage two the church is that agent: "To me . . . was given . . . to make all men see what is the plan of the mystery hidden for ages in God who created all things; that *through the church* the manifold wisdom of God might now be made known to the principalities and powers in the heavenly places."

Concerning the function of the *agape* life in the believer in Christ, St. Paul says: "God . . . through Christ reconciled us to Himself and gave us the ministry of reconciliation; that is, God was in Christ reconciling the world to Himself, not counting their trespasses against them, and entrusting to us the message of reconciliation. . . . We beseech you on behalf of Christ, be reconciled to God" (2 Cor. 5:18-20). God was reconciled to man through the self-sacrificing *agape* of Christ, and now through the new *agape* life in the believing Christian the ongoing work of reconciling man to God continues. With this in mind, what St. Paul wrote to the Colossians now begins to make sense: "I rejoice in my sufferings for your sake, and in my flesh *I complete what is lacking* in Christ's afflictions" (Col. 1:24). In other words, *the job was only half done when Christ died and rose again; it is completed as Christ in the Christian believer continues the* agape *life and thus extends it through people to people.*—Much of what is intended to be said within the covers of this book is expressed in this sentence.

To put it in different words, when Christ died and rose again from the dead, God reconciled the world to Himself. In that sense reconciliation is complete. But the reconciliation process continues. It is in this role that the people who are the church function. They bring Christ's reconciliation to those places geographically and in those times historically where and when Jesus has not as yet come in His saving grace through the Gospel.

The Mind of Christ—the Mind of His Followers

From the vantage point of a cell in the imperial prison in Rome, St. Paul wrote to the Christians of Ephesus about their new life in Christ. And well might he do it, for all that the Christian life implies was then being lived out in his life. On bended knee he prayed to God, petitioning Him in their behalf. He wanted them to have and to continue to grow in the *agape* life.

From what was conceivably a dark, dank, and stuffy dungeon, hidden from sunshine, fresh air, the song of birds, the fragrance of flowers, and the rustle of leaves, he was led by the Spirit of God not only to pray in lofty words for the saints in Ephesus, but by the same Spirit he was given power to write about the *agape* life. In so doing he wanted to lead those to whom he wrote to the mountaintop of high inspiration where they could see unfolded before the eyes of faith a picture of transcendent beauty—the *agape* life of the believer in Christ.

He wrote about his prayer to God in their behalf. The Christ of the *agape* was to take up His abode in their hearts through faith; they were to be firmly established, "rooted and grounded in *agape*"; by the wisdom which the Spirit of God alone can give they were "to comprehend," in fellowship "with all the saints," the *agape* in all its dimensions—length, breadth, height, and depth; they were to be brought into the innermost sanctuary of God, there to see unfolded before their gazing eyes the mystery of the ages: "the *agape* of Christ which surpasses knowledge." And in order that they might understand that this *agape* life is not a piecemeal giving of God, but the indivisible, infinite, and transcendent God Himself, a real incarnation, St. Paul concluded with these words, "that you may be filled with all the fullness of God." (See Eph. 3:14-19.)

As the *agape* of God was expressed in the self-giving and self-sacrificing life of Christ for men, so it is also expressed in the life of the Christian believer. The gift of the new *agape* life is not intended merely to make the Christian feel good all over as he contemplates the forgiveness of his sins, his restoration to sonship, membership in the divine family, and the sweet hope of heaven. All of this is intended, and much more. As far as his fellowman is concerned, the purpose of the new life in the Christian is that he give it to others in loving self-sacrifice.

Christian suffering is never merely the outcome of an irascible hostility imposed by godless men, nor is it the inexorable development of fate. When the Christian suffers as a Christian, he suffers because of his attitude toward God and his fellowman. This suffering is the result of an attitude of the mind. But it is not a purely human mental process. There is something divine in this mind process, something uniquely divine. It is the attitude of a divine mind, the mind of God incarnate in the man Christ, and now of God in the person of Christ incarnate in the believer. Christian suffering is the expression of a *new* mind in the Christian, the mind of Christ in the Christian.

When Christ was hanging on the cross, His enemies thought He was not able to save Himself (Mark 15:31); it was blind fate or the due reward of His deeds or another example of the overpowering might of those who were stronger than He. But Christ's suffering was the result of the attitude of the *agape* mind of God that was in Him. The suffering of Christ was due to the mind of Christ.

Since Christ doesn't have two minds, one that brought Him to the cross and one which, in His total self, is in the believing Christian, one must conclude that the new mind of the Christian is the mind of Christ; and it is this mind of Christ in the Christian that is expressed in Christian suffering.

That Christian suffering is an expression of the mind of Christ in the Christian believer cannot be thought of as a new theological formulation. It did not have its beginning with Bonhoeffer and other theologians of the 20th century, nor with Luther and many who preceded him; the New Testament itself is the original source of this theological concept.

St. Paul wrote to the Christians at Philippi that Christ "became obedient unto death, even death on a cross." In calling upon them to live out their new lives, he exhorted them, "Have this mind among yourselves, which you have in Christ Jesus" (Phil. 2:5). Throughout the Epistle to the Philippians St. Paul explicitly describes Christian suffering as an expression of the new mind. (2:2, 5; 3:15, 19; 4:7)

Faith in Christ, St. Paul says, is a gift bestowed by the Spirit of God. But a concomitant gift of the same Spirit is the ability to suffer for the sake of Christ (Phil. 1:29). Faith in Christ and suffering for Christ go hand in hand. They are related to each other as the fruit is related to the tree.

Faith and Christian suffering accompany each other on the pathway of the Christian life. This truth is not always fully appreciated; sometimes it is vigorously opposed. Among the more conservative churches there is an understandable and justifiable concern "for the faith which was once for all delivered to the saints" (Jude 3). These churches are on solid Biblical and apostolic ground when they insist that Christian faith is the principal thing; that without it man is still in darkness, without the light of life. And when they claim that Christian teaching in apostolic orthodoxy is essential to the establishment and propagation of the faith, they are once again on terra firma. But St. Paul would probably pooh-pooh the idea of doctrine for doctrine's sake. Doctrine? Yes; but doctrine for faith, and faith for life. And life involves suffering. These are St. Paul's words: "It has been granted to you that for the sake of Christ you should *not only believe in Him but also suffer for His sake*" (Phil. 1:29). Orthodox Christians, both clergy and laity, become very unorthodox if they, in one way or another, try to preserve the church by bypassing the suffering that may be inherent in a consistently faithful witness to the Christ who presents Himself to us in the person who is discriminated against, possibly because of the color of his skin or his ethnic background.

This capacity to suffer "for the sake of Christ" is of the very essence of the new *agape* life in the Christian. To bypass this suffering, no matter what the pretext or good intention, is a denial of the new life itself and as such a denial of Christ and of God.

Christ "came . . . to give His life as a ransom for many" (Matt. 20:28). To give His life for others was the planned purpose of His coming. For that reason He would not be deterred in His journey to death. He set His "face like a flint" (Is. 50:7). Even His friends were slow in catching on. After they had been in His presence and intimate association for several years, they still did not grasp the significance of His real calling and purpose. On one occasion "He said to them: 'Behold, we are going up to Jerusalem, and everything that is written of the Son of Man by the prophets will be accomplished. For He will be delivered to the Gentiles, and will be mocked and shamefully treated and spit upon; they will scourge Him and kill Him, and on the third day He will rise.' *But they understood none of these things; this saying was hid from them, and they did not grasp what was said.*" (Luke 18:31-34)

When His friends began to sense that He was in dead earnest about this going-to-death business, even they proved themselves to be less than cooperative. As ominous clouds of opposition were forming and Jesus indicated His intention to go into the neighborhood of the stronghold of His religious opponents, His disciples warned Him not to go because, they said, His enemies had made plans to stone Him. But when He would not be swerved from His purpose, one of them (possibly with sarcastic overtones) said, "Let us also go, that we may die with Him." (John 11:16)

On another occasion, when Jesus had again spoken in plain language concerning His mission on earth that was to take Him to the cross and the tomb, impetuous "Peter took Him and began to rebuke Him, saying, 'God forbid, Lord! this shall never happen to You.' But He turned and said to Peter, 'Get behind Me, Satan! You are a hindrance to Me; for you are not on the side of God, but of men.'" (Matt. 16:22-23)

And as it was with Christ, so it is with the Christian believer when he lives out his new life in Christ.

"I PREFER PEACE"

When Christ prepared His friends for discipleship, He told them in unequivocal language what it would cost:

> If any one comes to Me and does not hate his own father and mother and wife and children and brothers and sisters, yes, and even his own life, he cannot be My disciple. Whoever does not bear his own cross and come after Me cannot be My disciple. For which of you, desiring to build a tower, does not first sit down and count the cost, whether he has enough to complete it? Otherwise, when he has laid a foundation, and is not able to finish, all who see it begin to mock him, saying, "This man began to build, and was not able to finish." Or what king, going to encounter another king

> in war, will not sit down first and take counsel whether he is able with ten thousand to meet him who comes against him with twenty thousand? And if not, while the other is yet a great way off, he sends an embassy and asks terms of peace. (Luke 14:26-32)

On one occasion I addressed an audience, as I had often done before, on the nature of the new Christian life: that it involves giving oneself unselfishly in the interest of others. My audience was composed of members of a suburban congregation, property-owning, middle-class people who were enjoying the comforts and luxuries of our well-advanced American economy. They seemed to give assent to what I said about the nature of the new life that is ours through Christ. Without mincing words I told them that, having the life and the mind of Christ, we also have the gift of the Spirit to suffer for the sake of Christ. And when they apparently accepted that, I made application to the current race issue: They had the opportunity to live out their Christian lives by identifying themselves with members of the racial minority group who lived in the big city nearby, and one of the specific problems of the group was that, because of their racial identity, they were not able to move their families out of the ghettolike slum areas of the big city. A challenge to the faith of those whom I addressed, I said, would present itself when members of the minority group would try to buy or rent property outside the slum area, in the suburban community in which my audience lived.

After the formal lecture period and the less formal question-and-answer period, while many were sipping coffee, a woman realtor, who until then had remained silent, approached me. She wanted to tell me of the philosophy that she followed in her business. Altruistically, she sought the well-being of her clients. In selecting a neighborhood and a home for them, she bore in mind their need for peace, tranquility, and comfort. To move a family of another racial group into the community would unduly disturb the community and disrupt the peace; and she, the realtor, would inform any minority-group members who would want to move into the "peaceful" community—the maintenance of whose peace was to some degree her responsibility—that they themselves would be ostracized by the community; not only would the peace of the community be disturbed, but they too could not live there in peace. The realtor informed me that she had a feeling of compassion for the minority group, and that when, through an education process, the community was ready to accept minority group members, she would be glad to serve them.

But what the realtor spoke of was a pseudopeace, perhaps the peace that goes before the storm. She was crying, "'Peace, peace,' when there is [was] no peace" (Jer. 6:14). Peace without justice and equity is no peace at all. And to exclude people because of a different degree of skin pigmentation from enjoying the good things of creation—sunshine, space, adequate living quarters, and acceptance as human beings—is in the final analysis a rejection of the God who made them and of the God who became incarnate in the person of Jesus Christ.

Christ made a very clear-cut distinction between the "peace of God" and "peace without justice" when He told His disciples:

> Every one who acknowledges Me before men, I also will acknowledge before My Father who is in heaven; but whoever denies Me before men, I also will deny before My Father who is in heaven.
>
> Do not think that I have come to bring peace on earth; I have not come to bring peace, but a sword. For I have come to set a man against his father, and a daughter against her mother, and a daughter-in-law against her mother-in-law; and a man's foes will be those of his own household. He who loves father or mother more than Me is not worthy of Me; and he who loves son or daughter more than Me is not worthy of Me; and he who does not take his cross and follow Me is not worthy of Me. He who finds his life will lose it, and he who loses his life for My sake will find it. (Matt. 10:32-39)

The realtor was told that if these words of Christ—read in Christian churches and preached from Christian pulpits to Christian worshipers—are not to be spoken against them on the great Judgment Day, then they must be lived out in the lives of Christians, also Christian realtors as they ply their trade in the community. When she was reminded that Christ said, "I have not come to bring peace," she responded, "I prefer peace."

On another occasion a realtor was more blunt—perhaps more honest. During a similar conversation, he pulled out his wallet, laid it on the table, and said, "This is the reason we do what we do."

AS A LAMB TO THE SLAUGHTER

Another woman realtor responded quite differently to the challenge of witnessing to Christ in her business dealings. She had established herself in a Florida community, was doing well in her business, and was held in high esteem by her fellow realtors. Until something happened.

A client of another real estate broker owned a new, never-occupied house near a country club. A Negro doctor was interested in buying it. The broker, fearing a cross-burning if he sold it to the doctor, turned the matter over to the woman realtor. Her sensitive conscience urged her to show the house to the doctor. He decided he wanted it.

The realtor felt a need to build a social bridge between the doctor and his prospective neighbors, so she gave a dinner, inviting the owner of the house next door and about a dozen other people. It went off well. She visited the man across the street and the minister of the nearby church. She thought everything was working out beautifully until—telephone calls, anonymous letters, nearby property owners trying to buy the doctor out.

Her next experience was with the executive board of the local board of realtors. Since she was treasurer, they could not legally hold meetings without notifying her. But they insisted that she leave the room while they discussed the "problem." When her fellow realtors realized that she could not be intimidated, they began to ignore her. This gave them some difficulty since she was chairman of various committees and an officer.

Despite the code of ethics, said to begin by stating it is based on the Golden Rule, the ethics committee at an annual meeting of the local board of realtors recommended that her realtor's license be revoked, and the assembled group roundly approved the recommendation. After she confronted her critics by telling them how she happened to sell the house to the distinguished Negro doctor, enumerating his impressive accomplishments and the efforts she had put forth to create a spirit of welcome in the neighborhood, and after she had told them what her concept of ethical real estate practice was, she returned to her seat amid dead silence; and the president called for the next order of business.

At the national convention of the board of realtors, where she had requested a hearing, her former friends ignored her. New charges were cooked up back home and, though every effort was made to appeal the decision of the ethics committee, she was expelled from the board of realtors. After that she no longer sold real estate but took up work with the United Church of Christ in Philadelphia.[2]

When a Christian is faithful to his calling, cross bearing and suffering are inevitable. This may entail sacrifice—the sacrifice of prestige, honor, friendship, acceptance, and a livelihood—and in some cases life itself.

The Christian principle is what counts. All of God's good creation, the tangibles and the intangibles, when enjoyed by man are to be claimed and used by him upon the basis of justice toward his fellowman. And when the exigencies of the case call for the sacrifice of these good things of creation, the Christian will count the loss of them as gain (Phil. 3). This is the *agape* of God in the life of the true follower of Christ; and he will "count it all joy." (James 1:2)

NO CREPEHANGING

To interpret as negative and joy-killing a theology that spells out the nature of the new Christian life as self-sacrifice involving suffering for the sake of justice is a gross misunderstanding and a misinterpretation of the new life in Christ. Unless a person has masochistic tendencies, he need not turn away from Christianity as though it were a joy-killer or a dispenser of gloom. Though Christian theology has much to say about sadness and death, it has much more to say about joy and life. If it is a life that God alone can give and which comes to us in Christ, in the final analysis it must be the source of the only true joy. All cross bearing and suffering, even death itself, is preparatory for life to those who are in Christ. For in the *agape* life of God, bestowed by God through Christian baptism, we have Christ; and in Christ God's purpose in creation is restored, and with it real joy in the knowledge of God and service in His family to the glory and praise of God.

Christ was a "Man of sorrows and acquainted with grief" (Is. 53:3), yet He was to "see the fruit of the travail of His soul and be satisfied" (Is. 53:11). Though "He humbled Himself and became obedient unto death, even death on a cross. . . . God has highly exalted Him and bestowed on Him the name which is above every name, that at the name of Jesus every knee should bow, in heaven and on earth and under the earth, and every tongue confess that Jesus Christ is Lord, to the glory of God the Father" (Phil. 2:8-11). Sorrow, pain, suffering, and death, yes; but also joy in far greater measure – present already in contemplation of the grand consummation: the exaltation, and the restoration of the purpose of God in creation.

If a Christian crossbearer is tempted like Elijah to think that he walks alone down "the way of sorrows," he can be told that he is surrounded by others of similar loneliness; and in the midst of them all is the Christ Himself. Let the crossbearer look "to Jesus, the Pioneer and Perfecter of our faith, who *for the joy that was set before Him* endured the cross, despising the shame, and is seated at the right hand of the throne of God." (Heb. 12:2)

Because of the *agape* that was His, Christ could tell His disciples, in anticipation of His suffering, death, resurrection, and ascension: "Blessed are you that hunger now, for you shall be satisfied. Blessed are you that weep now, for you shall laugh. Blessed are you when men hate you, and when they exclude you and revile you, and cast out your name as evil, on account of the Son of Man! *Rejoice in that day, and leap for joy,* for behold, your reward is great in heaven; for so their fathers did to the prophets" (Luke 6:21-23). And this is St. Paul's response: "We suffer with Him [Christ] in order that we may also be glorified with Him" (Rom. 8:17). In commenting on this passage, Luther says: "He [St. Paul] turns his back to the world and his eyes toward the revelation which is to come, as though he could perceive no sorrow or affliction anywhere on earth, but only joy. Indeed, he says, when we do have to suffer evil, what is our suffering in comparison with the unspeakable joy and glory which shall be made manifest in us?" [3]

To bypass the suffering that may result from identifying oneself with the oppressed – in this case those who are deprived of justice and acceptance because they are members of racial or ethnic minority groups – by sacrificing the principle involved is a most dangerous procedure. At best a pseudohappiness can result: acceptance by one's peers, and the social and economic security resulting from imposing insecurity upon others. Unless it is repented of, that type of joy-seeking may indeed result in "wailing and gnashing of teeth," existentially and eschatologically, that is, here in time and hereafter in eternity; it can haunt by day and by night and rise up in just accusation before the judgment seat of God.

It is all wrapped in one bundle: (1) *the new life of God* which became incarnate in Jesus Christ and is given to man as a gift in Christian baptism; (2) *the extension of this new life to others*—in the area of concern of this book—by refusing to move out of the community when members of another racial or ethnic group move in, by identifying oneself with them, earnestly seeking their admission into the full fellowship of the church at the Communion table and in every aspect of congregational life and activity, and by working for even-handed justice that would rule out every type of racial or ethnic discrimination in the home community, the city, the state, the nation, and the world; and (3) *the joy that God alone can give.* This package deal which is ours through Christ is the new life of God, the giving of that life to others, and the joy that God gives us in the doing of it. It is the gift of the triune God: the life of God the Father is given to us through the death and resurrection of Jesus Christ—and through us to others; and the joy intended by God for man is ours through the Holy Spirit.

Building the Church on Principle

It is the responsibility of Christian people, identified with a local congregation or parish, to use all legitimate means at their disposal to carry on the work God has given to the church. It is a real blessing of God when members of the congregation contribute liberally to the work of the local parish and toward the work of the church at large. When they see the evident blessing of God resting upon their labors, in more people professing the faith, thus adding to the numerical strength of the congregation, they have reason to praise God and to take courage for greater and bolder undertakings intended to strengthen and to build the organized church. But institutional success made possible in an atmosphere of peace attained at any cost is not the purpose of God as He deals with men in and through the church.

The words of Christ at the close of the Sermon on the Mount may be applicable at this point:

> Every one then who hears these words of Mine and does them will be like a wise man who built his house upon the rock; and the rain fell, and the floods came, and the winds

> blew and beat upon that house, but it did not fall, because it had been founded on the rock. And every one who hears these words of Mine and does not do them will be like a foolish man who built his house upon the sand; and the rain fell, and the floods came, and the winds blew and beat against that house, and it fell; and great was the fall of it.
>
> And when Jesus finished these sayings, the crowds were astonished at His teaching, for He taught them as one who had authority, and not as their scribes. (Matt. 7:24-29)

It is the foundation that counts. The foundation is the principle expressed by Christ in these words: "A new commandment I give to you, that you love one another; even as I have loved you" (John 13:34). In giving His disciples the directive for building the institution of the church upon the foundation of the Christian principle, Christ said, "You shall be My witnesses" (Acts 1:8). In the final analysis, that is the Christian's total responsibility: to witness to Christ.

To witness to Christ means to acknowledge Him as Lord (1 Cor. 12:3). He is the Lord of life, the new life that man has through faith in Him. Witnessing to Christ covers the whole gamut of the Christian's life, his new existence. It is expressed in what he says and leaves unsaid; in what he does and leaves undone. His first responsibility, then, is not to build the institution, that is, the organized church. His first responsibility is not even to build *the* church, which in the Apostles' Creed is called "the communion of saints" and in the older versions of the Nicene Creed the "one holy Catholic and Apostolic Church."

A faithful witness to Christ is a witness to the whole Christ, to the Christ of Good Friday and Easter, to the Christ seated at the right hand of the Majesty on high (Heb. 1:3), but also the Christ who comes to man in the lowly, the outcast, and the despised (Matt. 25:31-46). Christ proclaimed the good news of the mercy and forgiveness of God, and we are to do so also. But to refuse to work for equal justice for all, with the lame excuse that what people need most is the Gospel—"the church's one responsibility is to preach the Gospel, to save souls"—is to deny the Christ who through His incarnation identified Himself with all men in their total need, "not ashamed to call them brethren" (Heb. 2:11), whose life is described in the words "He went about doing good." (Acts 10:38)

These are days of revolutionary change; and those who have

eyes to see and ears to hear can both see and hear that social and racial injustice is threatening to discredit the church and to destroy the nation. For the church and church people to stand on the sidelines as mere spectators can be diabolical hypocrisy because, though they make confession of Christ, they may be denying Him by refusing to become involved in the interest of justice in behalf of His brothers.

God's house is a house of prayer for all peoples (Is. 56:7). A faithful witness to Christ eliminates every possibility of a color bar in the organization and life of the church and of the local congregation. It is in the church that the universality of God's grace in Christ is proclaimed. It is in the church where the ecumenicity of the Gospel is confessed and where men and women are sought and enlisted to bring the good tidings of God's love in Christ to the ends of the earth so that all men seeing the salvation wrought by God might embrace it and thus become members of the community of the redeemed.

The Witness and the Inquiring Mind

Although success is of God and is not guaranteed to flow forth every time the church and church people witness faithfully to Christ, it is nevertheless then that Christ's prophecy is fulfilled, "that they may see your good works and give glory to your Father who is in heaven" (Matt. 5:16). Seeing "your good works" is what Friedrich Nietzsche called for in the words attributed to him: "Christians must first show me that they are redeemed before I will believe in their Redeemer."

The Honorable McCauley Peters Akpoyoware, then Second Secretary of the Nigerian Embassy in Washington, was one of the speakers at a human relations institute conducted on the campus of Valparaiso University. The theme of the institute was "Our Image Abroad." The institute was discussing the future of the church among the newly emerging nations of Africa. The discussion centered in the necessity of the church and its people, especially those missionaries to Africa representing Christianity in Europe and the U. S. A., to identify themselves with the African people in their total human need. Mr. Akpoyoware said, "If the Christian message is to be heard and accepted, there must first be an inquiring mind." People will want to know, if and when church people—in this case, missionaries and other church representatives—accept people as people, what is the high principle upon which the altruistic acceptance of them is based; what is the hidden power behind the good attitude and the unselfish deed?

There is an ever-growing segment of society to whom the church can address itself most effectively if the church and its people will in greater measure live out their new life in Christ as they seek to identify themselves with people in their total need, their total humanity. This is one of the great challenges that confronts the church in an age of sophistication without parallel in history.

REJECTION OF MAHATMA GANDHI

It was on Christmas Eve in the latter part of the 19th century that a young man came to a Christian church in Durban, in Natal Province, South Africa. Having studied in England, he was now in Durban practicing law. He was no professing Christian, but the New Testament was better known, used, and respected by him than by many professing the Christian faith, and he was impressed by the teaching, the life, and the person of Jesus Christ. Now he had come to a Christian church when the church was celebrating the anniversary of Christ's birth. He came intending in his way to join the congregation in its festive service and to honor the Man of whom the New Testament speaks. But he did not celebrate Christmas with the Christians, for he was turned away at the church door because he was of a different skin color. In trying to save themselves and perhaps their church, they were the instruments in the hands of the Evil One to turn away from the church Mahatma Gandhi, who became one of the greatest men that God has given to the world in the 20th century. Soon thereafter he returned to his native India, where, through long and unselfish suffering, he secured freedom from British rule for his people. What might have happened if he had been welcomed into the Christian fellowship of that Durban church on Christmas Eve!

LIGHT FOR THE GROPING

Faithful witness to Christ can be an instrument of the Spirit of God to win those who are groping about outside the Christian community, searching hopelessly for reality and meaning in life. But the same witness can be used by the Spirit of God to strengthen the weak and to bring back those standing on the brink of unbelief and spiritual disaster.

A woman had been won for the church. She rejoiced in her newly found faith and was grateful to God for the guidance of His Spirit and for the pastor of the church, who had taught her the way of life in Christ. But she was soon disillusioned. The pastor who had been instrumental in bringing her into the church became to her the source of an offense that all but drove her out again. Though he was concerned about her spiritual well-being, he seemed unconcerned about the needs of nonwhite newcomers who were moving into the community of the church. The human element that was instrumental in keeping her from forsaking the church and her newly found faith was a small association within the denomination. This organization had as its goal the eradication of every vestige of discrimination based on racial or ethnic differences.

A young man who had a deep concern for people in distress became dissatisfied with the church because in his opinion it was not addressing itself to the obvious, staggering, known needs of people. As a result, his contributions, running into hundreds of dollars yearly, rather than going to the work of the organized church, were channeled to secular organizations addressing themselves to the eradication of racial discrimination. When he heard that within his own denomination there was an organization functioning with the specific purpose of helping to remove discrimination based on racial or ethnic distinctions, he began to contribute from $500 to $800 annually toward the work of that association. Not only that. He later wrote to that association's executive, who had established meaningful communication with him: "It was your influence and that of your association that kept me from giving up the faith and completely turning away from Christianity and the church."

Another young man, a Ph. D. teaching at one of our renowned private universities, was disheartened when he found his home congregation making obeisance to the god of racial exclusion. He lost his Christian faith. Through the faithful witness to Christ against racial prejudice and discrimination on the part of a private association within the denomination of his former church connection, he returned to affiliate once again with the Christian community and to become a strong witness to Christ, helping to bring the church into the vanguard in human relations.

"DRAW ALL MEN TO ME"

A church that had already celebrated its 100th anniversary was situated in what had become one of the most cosmopolitan communities in the country. For decades it had satisfied itself with ministering only to "its own kind," while surrounded by human beings of "every nation and tribe and tongue and people" (Rev. 14:6) – Italians and Negroes, Puerto Ricans and Germans, Irish, Mexicans, and Greeks. But a young pastor took charge of the congregation with the determination that he would lead the congregation – what was left of it – to identify itself in its outreach and witness with all the people of the community in their total need. When a new program adapted to the needs of the people was in the process of development, members of the same church denomination living in other parts of the metropolis transferred their membership to the congregation; they wanted to have a part in the church's ministry where need was found, recognized, and ministered to. They themselves were enriched and no doubt began to understand the better what Christ meant when He said, "It is more blessed to give than to receive." (Acts 20:35)

A faithful witness to Christ wherever such witness is possible has its rewards; one becomes an instrument of the Spirit of God to win people for Christ, to restore the disillusioned, and to strengthen the faithful. But let it be said again: the building of the institution, the winning of some, and the saving of those already won is not the church's principal objective; a faithful witness to Christ *is*.

Neither Jew nor Greek, Neither Negro nor Indian

At the time of His incarnation Christ left His high throne in heaven, not considering it a matter of display to be equal with God (free translation of Phil. 2:6); but relinquishing His godly prerogative of transcendence, He identified Himself with poor, sin-debased mankind – all of it. No one could ever call a man "brother" (Heb. 2:11) in the same sense and to the full degree that Christ could as a result of His becoming man. He was God's gift to *the world* (John 3:16). He was "the Lamb of God who takes away the sin of *the world*" (John 1:29). In this sense He was neither Jew nor Gentile, Oriental nor Occidental, Mongoloid, Negroid, or Caucasoid. He was not provincial but cosmopolitan. He literally belonged to the world of human beings – to people of all times and climes. And having Christ in them, His witnesses in the world are His imitators (Eph. 5:1). In witnessing to Him, the world's one infinitely great Citizen, they become cosmopolitan themselves. In this sense and in this context they lay aside their provincial identification as Jew, Gentile, Westerner, German, Anglo-Saxon, Negro, Indian, or what-have-you. In fact, as they witness to Christ they give over to Him all of their former selves, both the bad and the good, so that the Christ in them becomes their new life.

BAD AND GOOD GIVEN TO CHRIST

He who faithfully witnesses to Christ, through daily contrition and repentance gives all the bad of his former self—his rebellion against the rule of God in his life—to Christ who, nailing it to the cross (Col. 2:14), becomes "the expiation" for his sins (1 John 2:2). Through Christ the witness to Christ becomes free from the bondage of egotistical self-service to become like Christ, God's free man, free to serve God by serving his fellowman in his total need.

When faithfully witnessing to Christ, the witness gives up also all that is good in him. This he places on the altar of God as a holy and acceptable sacrifice, a spiritual worship (Rom. 12:1). Among the good things that he brings to God in service to the world are his native and developed talents, whatever experience under Divine Providence is his, as well as the better elements of his tradition and culture. For example, while the church, in full recognition of much that is good in American Indian culture, in approaching the Indian must do so with the full impact of the new life in Christ, the Indian, in the acceptance of Christ, sacrifices his Indian-ness on the altar of God. Nothing more and nothing less must be required of him. He too must become a Christlike person, a "world citizen."

INDIAN-NESS

It is generally admitted among knowledgeable churchmen that one of the major mistakes the church has made in its approach to the Indian was the attempt either consciously or otherwise to equate Christianity with our inherited European culture; an Indian Christian was a good Christian to the extent that he mimicked us in all our cultural traits. But a greater danger confronting the church in witnessing to the Indian (and for that reason failing meaningfully to communicate to him) is the danger of paternalistically placing him on a pedestal, making a little demigod out of him. As a Christian who lives his life to the praise of God, the Indian in a sense ceases to be what he was—an Indian; he is a member of the body of Christ. In this sense, all provincial or ethnic inheritances disappear. That is what St. Paul is talking about when he says, "As many of you as were baptized into Christ have put on Christ. There is neither Jew nor Greek, there is neither slave nor free, there is neither male nor female; for you are all one in Christ Jesus" (Gal. 3:27-28). This is radical language. But it is only in radical challenge that men's hearts can be moved to accept the radical change of a new life.

THE HURT-EXPERIENCE

What are the good things with which the Negro comes into the kingdom of God, there to deposit whatever there is of value in his life as a sacrifice (Rom. 12:1) on the altar of God? In the first place, the native and developed talents he has received from the hand of the Creator. A Ralph Bunche can contribute his gift of diplomacy; Percy Julian, the chief developer of cortisone, his scientific know-how; Marian Anderson, her art as one of the world's great singers; Martin Luther King, Jr., his ability to make the social implications of the Gospel of Christ, by his eloquence and facile pen, heard and understood by untold millions; and the sharecropper of Fayette County, Tenn., can bring to the altar his courage as he tries to register and vote in the face of threats to his economic status and his very life.

But what shall the Negro do with his experience resulting from the ignorance, pride, and prejudice of his segregationist neighbors? —and there is no Negro in the United States old enough to understand who has not had such experiences. He has them daily; they come into his life overtly or subtly, or vicariously by means of the many media of communication. What shall the Negro, as he witnesses to Christ, do with these experiences? Surely the way of Richard Wright, Louis Lomax, James Baldwin, Dick Gregory, Stokeley Carmichael, and the Black Muslims is not the only answer. Cynicism and bitterness—though they may be a part of the unfolding picture of God acting in history, revealing His divine judgment upon unjust, self-seeking man—is not the use to which the Negro witnessing to Christ will put his experience. Though he may join those in Washington, Jackson, Chicago, Albany, Birmingham, Selma, or Milwaukee in civil rights demonstrations, thus lending his aid to those who would rid the land of rampant racial injustice, he will nevertheless accept the hurt of prejudice, discrimination, and segregation as an expression of Divine Providence, though at the time it is inflicted it may seem to be inscrutable.

In accepting the hurt as a divine blessing in disguise, the offended Negro will let God be God, "King of kings and Lord of lords." And when he cannot quite understand the circumstance in which he finds himself, he will say with St. Paul: "In everything God works for good with those who love Him" (Rom. 8:28). As a witness to Christ the Negro Christian will not look upon the hurt-experience as something that he must merely meekly and passively endure. It must be used by him in the service of his fellowman and to the glory of God.

It is the offended one that knows best the truly satanic nature of the offense; for he has experienced it in body, mind, and spirit. As James Baldwin says, "That man who is forced each day to snatch his manhood, his identity, out of the fire of human cruelty that rages to destroy it knows, if he survives his effort, and even if he does not survive it, something about himself and human life that no school on earth—and, indeed, no church—can teach." [4] He can deal with the offense and the offender as an authority. Having been called into the kingdom of God through the acceptance of the new life in Christ, he, like Christ, now becomes the dispenser of the blessing of God. He now uses his hurt-experience for constructive purposes by working toward the removal of the offense and by helping the one causing the hurt to turn from his wicked way and live. (Ezek. 33: 7-19)

It is not surprising that the great majority of the members of the National Association for the Advancement of Colored People, the National Urban League, the Southern Christian Leadership Conference, and other organizations dedicated to the elimination of racial discrimination and segregation are Negroes and that many of the leaders in these organizations are Negroes: Roy Wilkins, Whitney M. Young, Jr., and Martin Luther King, Jr.[5] They themselves have felt the hurt of racial discrimination. They can work most effectively to proclaim the true nature of "liberty throughout the land" (Lev. 25:10). It is they who can lay the sin upon the consciences of whites who have remained silent while race-baiting demagogues get themselves elected and reelected, and the disgrace that has been upon us for decades still cries to the heavens for elimination.

It is incumbent upon the Negro Christian to be in the vanguard in the struggle for racial justice and equality; and it is to the credit of many Negro ministers of the Gospel that they are identifying themselves by word and deed with the struggle and are thus setting a good example for their parishioners to follow.

Both the oppressed and the oppressor are to be helped; and the Negro Christian, upon whom the heavy hand of the oppressor is keenly felt, is prepared by the God of history to help the oppressor as no one else can.

Martin Luther King, Jr., in a sermon written in a Birmingham jail, said:

> With every ounce of our energy we must continue to rid this nation of the incubus of segregation. But we shall not in the process relinquish our privilege and our obligation to love. While abhorring segregation, we shall love the segregationist.
>
> To our most bitter opponents we say: "We shall match your capacity to inflict suffering by our capacity to endure suffering. We shall meet your physical force with soul force. Do to us what you will, and we shall continue to love you. We cannot in all good conscience obey your unjust laws, because non-cooperation with evil is as much a moral obligation as is cooperation with good. Throw us in jail, and we shall still love you. Bomb our homes and threaten our children, and we shall still love you. Send your hooded perpetrators of violence into the community at the midnight hour and beat us and leave us half dead, and we shall still love you. But be ye assured that we will wear you down by our capacity to suffer. One day we shall win freedom, but not only for oursIves. We shall so appeal to your heart and conscience that we shall win *you* in the process, and our victory will be a double victory." [6]

When the Negro Christian witnesses faithfully to Christ, he will pray and work in the interest of the oppressor, thus accepting the challenge found in the words of St. Paul: "Beloved, never avenge yourselves, but leave it to the wrath of God; for it is written, 'Vengeance is Mine, I will repay, says the Lord.' No, 'if your enemy is hungry, feed him; if he is thirsty, give him drink; for by so doing you will heap burning coals upon his head.' Do not be overcome by evil, but overcome evil with good." (Rom. 12:19-21)

Not all Negroes are sufficiently patriotic or enlightened or Christian to use their experience to help eradicate racial discrimination. To deny that discrimination is found also among Negroes and to deny that many Negroes could do more to help raise the standard of living among Negroes in general would be equivalent to denying the Biblical doctrine of original sin. Since there is one sinful human nature common to man, one must assume that, if environmental factors are the same, the sins found in white society may be anticipated to crop up among Negroes as well.

A necessary precaution must be exercised by non-Negroes who are guilty of being involved in the oppression imposed upon Negroes. It would be arrogant presumption to try to tell them what they should do to remove the problem which we ourselves have brought upon them and us. It would nevertheless be a disservice to Negro Christians, while discussing a theology for the church as it faces the worldwide race issue, not to speak of their high calling in Christ. This calling includes the use of the specific talent God has given them—the hurt-experience—conceived in the womb of centuries of pain, which constitutes a talent that they alone possess. "Stir up the gift of God which is in thee" (2 Tim. 1:6 KJV). When Negro Christians are called upon to place this specific talent of their experience as a "living sacrifice" upon the altar of God to be used by Him in His service, it is the prophets, the apostles, and Christ Himself who are asking them to do so.

To deny our differences of whatever kind is folly and involves a denial of creation and the Creator. To give our God-given differences back to the God who created them by using them according to His purpose for the well-being of mankind and to His glory is a high form of worship. The restoration of God's purpose in creation is realized in and through us by the power of the new life He has given us in Christ. To live out this new life, whether the Christian is Jew or Greek, slave or free, male or female, Indian, Negro, or European, is quite revolutionary. Christianity is revolutionary.

6

Christianity: the Great Revolution

See, I have set you this day over nations and over kingdoms to pluck up and to break down, to destroy and to overthrow, to build and to plant.

Jer. 1:10

At Loggerheads with the World

That Christianity is a revolutionary force let loose in the world should be obvious to anyone who honestly acquaints himself with the New Testament, with the life of Christ and His apostles, and with the church of the apostolic and postapostolic eras.

Christ was no complacent, me-too, status-quo fellow who wanted peace at any price. He came to overthrow the rule of wrong, the rule of sin. In doing so He became the Revolutionary *par excellence.* This was evident throughout His life. This revolutionary spirit took Him to the cross and the tomb. His rule as the Head of this divine revolution had its beginning and symbol in the wilderness temptation. (Matt. 4:1-11)

From the wilderness He went into the courts of the temple, into the homes of people, and out on the dusty roads of Palestine. The spirit of revolution was evident in what He did, in what He said, and in where He chose to go. It wasn't long before some men caught on; they understood that He had come to revolutionize and to establish a new rule and a new kingdom among men. They wanted Him to be a bread king, but He refused. Some perhaps would have liked to have Him join them in their hopes and plans to overthrow the power of their great political enemy, Caesar, and to establish Himself as their ruler *to their glory.* Although He possessed all authority in heaven and on earth (Matt. 28:18), He nevertheless said, "My kingdom is not of this world." (John 18:36)

The end of the revolutionary is very often death. Christ, the great Revolutionary, was no exception. With dogged determination the religious leaders of His day planned to get Him; and get Him they did, while secular rulers acquiesced, and many yelled, "Crucify Him, crucify Him!" And crucify Him they did.

The same fate awaited His friends, His fellows in the great revolution. Before they could join His ranks, they were told to count the cost. And this was the cost—to give up their old life and to be born anew (John 3:3). What could be more revolutionary than that?

When they had been immersed in this revolutionary spirit, they defied the consequences to their physical well-being as they told their judges that the word and work of the revolution must go on: "Whether it is right in the sight of God to listen to you rather than to God, you must judge; for we cannot but speak of what we have seen and heard" (Acts 4:19-20). As the revolution moved from victory to victory, those who opposed it were compelled to admit its power. They said of the revolutionaries that they had "turned the world upside down." (Acts 17:6)

When opposition to the revolution became overt and full blown, while one of its lieutenants (apostles) after another was thrown into prison and some of them were killed, these revolutionaries "went everywhere, preaching the word" (Acts 8:4 KJV) of the revolution. Thousands of them became heroes of the revolution and martyrs for Christ. The army of the revolution (the church) met its Commander-in-chief in Word and Sacrament to learn His strategy and to be strengthened by Him; and the meeting place in some instances was the catacombs. From there they marched forth to glorious victory in the Roman arena.

When true to itself, Christianity is often at loggerheads with the world and with any specific social environment within that world from which it has been set free. That is its nature.

The author of *The Church in Disrepute*[1] calls Christ the "arch-rebel" and accuses the church of underestimating and permitting its ministers to underestimate "the seriousness of the Christian adventure and the cost thereof."

When men claim Christianity as their faith but explicitly or implicitly deny the revolutionary nature of the faith they profess, they have already abandoned Christianity or are in great danger of doing so. Since there are moral and ethical matters involved in the modern race issue, Christianity must be involved in the issue; and if it is not involved, those who claim to be Christian are in danger of losing their Christianity, or they have already lost it. Christ is the Head of the revolution, and anyone bearing His name (if he is not a renegade, an apostate, or a quisling) must find himself in the battle and always on the side of the revolutionary forces. And *forces* they are.

Is Force a Farce?

"You can't use force."

"Force will do more harm than good."

"You defeat the very cause for which you are working when you use force."

Expressions of this kind represent the reaction of many people when a vigorous attempt is made to espouse the cause of minority groups. The assumption is, of course, that force is being used, a force that is not only harmful to the cause but also of an illegal and rebellious nature and, in the realm of the church, contrary to an evangelical approach.

As a parish pastor and later as the executive secretary of a church-related human relations association and as an editor, I have for many years been engaged in lecturing and writing on the race issue, especially as it affects the life and work of the church; I have also participated in certain civil rights demonstrations. As a result of these activities, much correspondence dealing with race relations has crossed my desk. Perhaps the most persistent criticism that has been made against my activities is the accusation that "you are using force to accomplish your purposes." May it be said to the credit of my critics that in almost all instances their criticisms were made in defense of what they thought to be a Christian approach.

Here are a few quotations culled at random from my files:

"I think you should be reprimanded for this most unchristian activity. I am wholeheartedly in favor of helping the colored race, *but not by violence* . . . inciting race riots, etc. We must first help their souls and in turn their bodies will be helped. Did our Lord and Savior Jesus Christ incite riots against social injustices of His day? Did He try to bring about social changes by *breaking laws?* Did He bring forth righteousness from unrighteous acts?"

"Only the cross can change the hearts of men. . . . It cannot be done by raising their social standards. Use the only power that God has given you, the power of His Word, to change the hearts of all men, both white and colored. Pay more attention to saving their souls instead of their bodies, and then only will this problem be resolved. You can never erase hate by *forcing* civic righteousness."

"It is high time for clergymen of all denominations to discontinue their participation in inciting disorder, revolt, and rebellion."

"I believe a Christian and intelligent approach and study of the problem in all fairness to both sides and without any *show of force* or violation of the law will accomplish the desired results."

"Doing what you are doing [participating in a demonstration in the interest of civil rights] places you in the same class as those whom you call lawbreakers. In fact, it places you below them, for they do not in many cases call themselves Christian."

"I don't know how informed you are on communism, but I say

forced integration is nothing but another means of taking away individual liberty."

"Why should you go to the South to stimulate insurrection?"

"Let no one say that we need an outside '*force*' to integrate the church."

"Yours was not a witness of love and concern, but rather one of *force*."

TWO TYPES OF FORCE

In order properly to evaluate the "force" criticism, it is necessary to remember that there are two types of force. It is force that does evil and it is force that accomplishes good. These two, as long as the earth remains, remain in mortal combat. St. Paul found both at work within himself. In his Letter to the Romans he describes the very nature of this conflict as he found it in himself:

> I do not understand my own actions. For I do not do what I want, but I do the very thing I hate. Now if I do what I do not want, I agree that the law is good. So then it is no longer I that do it, but sin which dwells within me. For I know that nothing good dwells within me, that is, in my flesh. I can will what is right, but I cannot do it. For I do not do the good I want, but the evil I do not want is what I do. . . . For I delight in the law of God, in my inmost self, but I see in my members another law at war with the law of my mind and making me captive to the law of sin which dwells in my members. (Rom. 7:15-19, 22-23)

And finally the great apostle says in victory, the victory of the force of good over the force of evil: "Thanks be to God through Jesus Christ our Lord!" (v. 25); I am delivered!

Before our nation and the church were conscious of a race problem in our own country and as it is found in the entire world today, there was a race problem. But it did not come into existence of itself. There was a very active power, the force for evil, that originated, maintained, and developed it. This force imposed by the dominant group upon people—because of certain biological traits such as skin pigmentation, hair texture, cranial measurements, and the like—resulted in the practice of all kinds of discrimination. By means of these discriminations people are denied equal justice and equal opportunity; this denial brings upon them the loss of the necessities of life and in many instances brutality and death. Above all, discrimination robs them of the God-given right to human dignity, the right to be human. This type of force is imposed by segregation-minded demagogues, by men of commerce and industry who have itching hands, by the lowly who have nothing else of which to be proud than that they are "white," and by the naively fearful.

This force sometimes is obvious, overt, and spelled out in vicious words and deeds. It is being used by Southern reactionaries who are opposing the mandates of the Supreme Court to open the polls to all citizens and to open all schools to all children. South of the Mason-Dixon line force has been used these many decades to "keep the Negro in his place"—the force of state laws which would deprive Negro citizens of rights guaranteed by the Constitution and especially by the Fourteenth and Fifteenth Amendments; the force of community attitudes that would compel Negroes to forego their natural and legitimate rights, and keep them in constant fear of the loss of their lives and their possessions. Force is being used by the so-called White Citizens Councils: the threat of the loss of jobs, of business, of property, if Negroes exercise their privilege as citizens by voting or if they express themselves as favoring the decision of the Supreme Court to abolish segregation in the public schools. All this is "force," contrary to good, ethical standards and contrary to our boasted American democracy.

Some respectable social scientists claim that the majority of Southerners are at heart opposed to racial discrimination and that those who foster segregation and discrimination are the political demagogues, the vicious, the illiterate, and those who have nothing else to boast about excepting the color of their skin. Yet the sad fact is that when good intentions are expressed in nothing but silence, the silence itself becomes a force to bolster the segregational status quo.

Christ has already given first-class citizenship in His kingdom to all believers. Theirs is the privilege of fellowship in the church with all its attendant responsibilities—privileges of corporate worship and of Holy Communion, the use of all the educational facilities of the church; responsibilities of working together in the local church, in congregational activities, and in the joint efforts of the church at large in its worldwide evangelization program. It is the God-intended purpose that through the Gospel ministry both the privileges and responsibilities of membership in the kingdom of

God should be conferred on those who believe. To try to resist this natural development of the Kingdom by endeavoring to withhold from people that which Christ has already given them is using force of the worst kind. It is resisting Christ and the work of His Spirit. And resisting the Spirit of God who awakens in believers the desire to be together in the fellowship of the church is force of a very potent kind. But seeking such fellowship is obedience to the prompting of the Spirit, whose power is thus made manifest.

THE GOSPEL IS DYNAMITE (Rom. 1:16)

It must be said with candor that force is being used in the interest of better race relations outside the church and in it. The struggle in the interest of the good is not carried on in a vacuum, so to speak; it is not shadowboxing, "beating the air" (1 Cor. 9:26). It is not a fantasy in which an imagined enemy is engaged in battle. It is rather the force for good confronting and engaging the force for evil.

Within the confines of human fallibility, the National Association for the Advancement of Colored People investigates what it considers un-American practices and the use of illegal pressures to keep from people their rights as citizens. When this association pleads before the courts the cause of those against whom discrimination is practiced, it is calling upon the government to use its God-given, legitimate powers—force—to gain justice for the oppressed. But force that is intrinsically objectionable because it is illegal is impossible on the part of minorities or those working in their interest. John Brown, the abolitionist, tried it at Harpers Ferry in 1859; although there were many slave uprisings, the unlettered slaves somehow knew better; they did not follow John Brown's plans for armed rebellion.

Truth can be a great power to change men's minds and to affect their consciences. Both the Law and the Gospel, if properly taught and applied to this area of men's lives, can be a mighty power (or force). According to conservative Reformation theology there is a valid distinction between the force inherent in law and legal procedures in the kingdom of the left hand, and the force with which the Gospel works; even though both of them have force, they are radically different forces. As the Christian witnesses to Christ, he will use both the Law and the Gospel. The Law of God will convict men of their sinful discriminatory practices; the Gospel will remold their lives and remove the blind spot in their Christianity, which in this instance is racial prejudice and discrimination. The very essence of Christian education and Christian witness is involved in what detractors have called "force."

There is another facet of this discussion of force which brings us to the heart of the Christian Gospel. It was force indeed, the power of the eternal, almighty God, that was involved in His coming into this world in the person of Jesus Christ. The powers of darkness had established the status quo of sin's rebellion against God. But that power was overthrown by Christ. How He did it was expressed by Him in these words: "I have come down from heaven, not to do My own will but the will of Him who sent Me" (John 6:38). This power was used by Christ in His public ministry when, by means of a whip, He cast out of the temple those who were there for the purpose of ungodly gain. When He turned to the self-righteous, Old Testament-quoting, Christ-denying advocates of the power of the Law for salvation, He called them "hypocrites" (Matt. 23:23), "serpents . . . brood of vipers" (Matt. 23:33), "of your father the devil" (John 8:44). The greatest force of all in the life of Christ as He walked visibly among men was His gathering into Himself the judgment of God upon sin. The power of the cross removed the wrath of God and with it sin and guilt. This was power indeed, the force of love pitted against the forces of evil.

This power is ours in and through the Son of God now risen from the dead and exalted at the right hand of God: "All power is given unto Me in heaven and on earth. Go . . . I am with you" (Matt. 28:18-20 KJV). He had power over the forces of evil. Now He had invested His lowly followers with that power, and they went, and force was pitted against force. They "filled Jerusalem" with His teaching (Acts 5:28). And when threatened by the force of legal power illegally used, they said, "We cannot but speak" (Acts 4:20), and they rejoiced "that they were counted worthy to suffer shame for His name" (Acts 5:41 KJV). Their blood became the seed of the church.

When the segregationist confronts the advocate of civil rights with the accusation, "You are using force," he is quite right. When the Christian is faithful to his calling, the power of the new life is at work against the forces of darkness.

Gradually—or Now?

Mary of Bethany "sat at Jesus' feet" as an attentive listener, drinking in the words of divine wisdom that flowed from His lips. He praised her for it. At the same time Martha, the sister of Mary, in good, matronly fashion, bestirred herself to serve Him; He reproved her for it. (Luke 10:38-41)

There is a time for serving God through action, and there is a time for serving God by silent, quiet listening. The time to be quiet is when God speaks. Truly God-pleasing Christian activity is always preceded by worship, quiet meditation, and prayer. It is in the silent presence of God that the human spirit is recharged and moved to action.

The action is in the service of Christ. The time for action is when Christ comes in a human brother. Waiting for a more convenient or auspicious occasion is sheer faithlessness, a rejection of the brother, of the God who created, and of the Christ who redeems. It can be devilish circumvention, then, to say: "Give the Holy Spirit a chance"; "You must educate first"; "You can't change things overnight"; "People's hearts must first be changed."

Both Mary and Martha are needed in the kingdom of God—in the church, too. In fact, the two personalities must be merged into one person. For both education and action are essential ingredients of the Christian way of life.

Education *and* action. But what is the proper chronological sequence? It may be well to throw that question out and get busy on both right now. Education now and action now!

An example from the life of Christ: The twelve-year-old Christ Child was found by Mary and Joseph in the temple, sitting among the theologians, listening to them and asking them questions. Mary and Joseph took Him by the hand and led Him out of the halls of learning, back to humble Nazareth and the carpenter shop of Joseph. That the educational process continued thereafter may be gleaned from the words, "Jesus increased in wisdom." But the obedience—action—did not await the completion of the learning process: "He went down with them and came to Nazareth and was obedient to them." (Luke 2:41-52)

To deny that citizens of the United States and members of the church are in need of more education in the area of race relations would be folly. But to wait until the educational process is completed—whenever that is—would be catastrophic. The one must be done and the other not left undone. While talking about the rightness of justice, equity, and fraternity, they must be practiced.

Such action cannot be postponed because human life is involved in all of it: the life of the oppressor and the life of the oppressed. Action needed now to save the church and the nation cannot wait even though some oppose being educated, some are slow in absorbing learning, and no one has emerged with all answers in his pocket. And action itself is an educational process, a very potent one; sometimes it is a better process than formal education. A. Philip Randolph said, "Mass demonstrations against Jim Crow are *worth a million editorials and orations in anybody's paper, on any platform.*" [2]

No knowledgeable, self-respecting, responsible person who day by day is subjected to the hurts and humiliations of a system of segregation and discrimination could be willing to accept gradualism as a policy. If he did, he would be denying his humanity and the dignity that is his as one of God's human creatures. Those who reject gradualism as a policy for the realization of acceptance, equity, and justice have no delusions as to the existence of gradualism. They know that traveling on the road toward the eradication of discrimination has been and probably will continue to be tortuously slow and painful.

In November 1945 the *Negro Digest* presented a symposium on gradualism. In it one of the contributors had this to say: "Racial equality . . . must be the immediate goal, just as a touchdown is always the immediate goal of a football team. It is the opposition of the opposing team that makes the advance of the ball gradual, a few yards at a time."

JUSTICE DEMANDS THE "NOW"

The desire for acceptance, equity, and justice is woven into the warp and woof of our being; it is a part of our creatureliness. God made us that way and, justifiably so, we want what He wants us to have, and we want it *now!*

At this point it is not necessary to present only Christian theology to show the validity of our argument. We can quote the New Testament and Christ Himself, "Whatever you wish that men would do to you, do so to them" (Matt. 7:12). Similar passages could be adduced from other religions to support this premise:

Taoism: "Regard your neighbor's gain as your own

gain, and regard your neighbor's loss as your own loss."

Confucianism: "What you do not want done to yourself, do not do to others."

Judaism: "Thou shalt love thy neighbor as thyself."

Islam: "No one of you is a believer until he loves for his brother what he loves for himself." [3]

Any person following the instinct of natural law can arrive at the same conclusion; a Christian, a Jew, a Buddhist, a Moslem, or even an agnostic or an atheist could conceivably render a just verdict in this matter if he occupied the chair of the judge in a court of justice. Justice always demands the "now." A judge is not satisfied with a promise from the murderer to murder less frequently until he gradually gives up murdering altogether. The judge is not content with a promise from the bank robber that he will gradually give up robbing banks. And a Christian congregation that still retains and exercises the authority to discipline an unrepentant member, when confronting a man with the sin of adultery, is not satisfied with a promise on the part of the sinner in question to reduce the sinning from a weekly to a monthly act and then to a bimonthly one, until he has gradually come to the point of giving it up altogether. Repentance is the killing of the old man, not a dying by easy stages.

Robbery robs man of tangible, physical possessions; racism would rob him of the dignity of being human. Adultery is sin against one's own body and that of another person. Racism, however, is a sin against a whole group of people with whom Christ has identified Himself through His incarnation. To put off sinning gradually, until all the "innocent" ones are educated or until the race baiters are ready to give up their race-baiting, in other words, to accept gradualism as a policy, is not a responsible stance in society in general and in the church in particular. Justice is not a commodity we can dole out according to our whims. It is a gift of God to those whom He has created, and the recognition of His rule is always expressed by man when he says *now* is the time for justice to "roll down." (Amos 5:24)

7

The Two Kingdoms

Render to Caesar the things that are Caesar's
and to God the things that are God's.

Luke 20:25

A Dual Citizenship

While Christianity is in its very nature revolutionary, it nevertheless offers peace here and now and actually gives it to those who will accept it. It is what St. Paul calls "the peace of God, which passes all understanding." (Phil. 4:7)

When a person becomes a Christian through faith in Christ, he enters into an entirely new relationship with God. He becomes a reconciled child of God. His sins are forgiven; his rebellion against the Creator has been pardoned. He is now in a state of divine grace. God now rules in the Christian's life not according to retribution but by grace, which is divine, unmerited favor. This is the rule of grace or the kingdom of grace. This is God's new rule which was effected through the death and resurrection of Jesus Christ.

In at least two of His parables Jesus made clear the nature of God's rule of grace. In the parable of the Laborers in the Vineyard (Matt. 20:1-16) He pictures this rule. The laborers expected to be paid according to the rule of reward or retribution, but the owner of the vineyard paid them according to a different principle: the generosity of his heart. In the parable of the Unmerciful Servant (Matt. 18:23-35) Jesus taught the same lesson. The steward owed his king ten thousand talents. Upon the request of the steward for time to repay the debt, the king "out of pity for him . . . released him and *forgave* him the debt." Jesus said, "The kingdom of heaven may be compared" with the king in his gracious, forgiving rule.

With the coming of Christ there are two kingdoms in which God rules. Several names have been given to both. The one has been called the kingdom of Christ, the kingdom of grace, and the kingdom of the right hand. The other, established by God in the order of creation, has been called the kingdom of the world, the kingdom of retribution, the kingdom of the left hand. Through the new covenant in Christ in Holy Baptism a man enters into a new relationship with God—God is reconciled to him; he is living in a state of grace, of forgiveness. But he is still a man, that is, a creature of God; therefore *he is in both kingdoms.*

From the kingdom of the right hand he receives life and all the blessings God intended for man in the creation. As a Christian he is a new creation. And, as St. Paul says, he is God's "new" workmanship, created in Christ Jesus *for good works* (Eph. 2:10). Although through his new grace-relationship to God he is "not of the world," he is nevertheless "in the world." Once again he is man in the truest sense; he is man who is a "little less than God" (Ps. 8:5). With all the prerogatives and all the potential as God's new creation, he can now move about in the world, the kingdom of the left hand, as God's new gift to the world, to restore it and all creation to God's original purpose.

THE SPIRITUAL BATTERY

While in the kingdom of the right hand the spiritual battery is recharged, in the kingdom of the left hand it is discharged. There the new man in Christ spends and is spent. Out in the world where people are, where poverty, disease, inequity, and injustice are to be found, the new man in Christ is to give his new life back to God, and his body a living sacrifice, "holy and acceptable to God" as his "spiritual worship" (Rom. 12:1). Wherever people are in need of help, there the Christian must be found bringing the *psychic* stuff of creation—justice and equity—as well as the *physical* things of God's good earth, to those who are in need. Though the new man in Christ enters into and is sustained in his new relationship to God by God's grace in the kingdom of the right hand, he is now called upon to do battle with the Evil One for the salvation of others, that the kingdom of this world should now become "the kingdom of our Lord and of His Christ" (Rev. 11:15). For as it was with Christ, so it must be with the followers of Christ.

He was tempted to fulfill His mission on earth by bypassing the cross and avoiding the conflict: by commanding stones "to become loaves of bread"; by throwing Himself down from "the pinnacle of the temple," as the real superman, for the acclaim of those assembled in the courts below; and by accepting "all the kingdoms of the world and the glory of them" by paying the easy price of a little "inoffensive" devil worship, which is a bypassing of the cross.

On another occasion the same tempter came to Christ in the person of His human enemies as they asked Him, "Is it lawful for us to give tribute to Caesar, or not?" (Luke 20:22). By a "yes" or "no" answer Christ was to deny either the kingdom of the right hand or the kingdom of the left hand; and to have denied either one would have been a denial of His mission on earth, that is, God's intention of restoring creation through the redemption.

In His answer to the "Is it lawful?" Jesus said, "Render to Caesar the things that are Caesar's, and to God the things that are God's" (Luke 20:25). The state, here referred to as Caesar, has its definite limitations. It must confine itself to the temporal well-being of man. The state violates its God-ordained purpose when in one way or another it tries to do the work of the kingdom of the right hand. That is the prerogative of the Spirit of God alone, and of those to whom God has given His Spirit, that is, the church. In the final analysis, the eradication of prejudice, with all its psychological reactions to the race issue, is outside the realm of the state; the segregationists and others are right when they claim that prejudice cannot be legislated out of, and love into, men's lives. It is the Spirit of God alone who can make new creatures out of old ones, for prejudice and lovelessness are of the nature of man in his fallen state. All the king's horses and all the king's men—in this instance the three branches of our Federal Government, with the power of executive order, Supreme Court pronouncements that favor justice, and laws to enforce it—cannot put Humpty Dumpty—man alienated from God and his neighbor—together again. The state, and for that matter the whole of the kingdom of the left hand, has its definite limitations in its functions in the interest of man's well-being. But the converse is not true. In His words "Render to Caesar the things that are Caesar's, and to God the things that are God's," Christ did not—and we cannot—set a limit to "the things that are God's."

All things in both kingdoms belong to God. But the usurper of God's throne, whom Christ called "the prince of this world" (John 14:30 KJV), and all his diabolical cohorts are apparently in temporary control of things in the kingdom of the left hand. However, Christ has already overcome them, and His kingdom and power and glory will be completely revealed at His second coming.

God has not abdicated, neither are the sons of God to abdicate their God-given prerogative of working in the kingdom of the left hand for the restoration of all of creation to its God-intended purpose. That justice may "roll down like waters, and righteousness like an everflowing stream" (Amos 5:24), and to the end that all of God's human creatures may stand upright in the dignity of those who were made in the likeness of God (Gen. 1:26-31), Christians too must be about their Father's business. The power (2 Cor. 12: 9-10), the enlightenment (Matt. 5:14), and the new life (John 14:6) that the Christian has received in the kingdom of the right hand he is to bring with him into the kingdom of the left hand "for the healing of the nations." (Rev. 22:2)

Politics and Government—a Christian Concern

Man is empowered by grace for action in the kingdom of the left hand. The Christian has opportunity and a responsibility to exercise his newly acquired faith and life in every conceivable circumstance in the world in which he lives, in all social relations, in business, industry, labor, and—in an area of specific concern in the context and purpose of this chapter—government and politics.

Human nature being what it is, politics and government often fall far short of God's purpose. The result is injustice, with God's purpose in creation thwarted. Under such circumstances the involvement of the Christian man is both a theological and a practical necessity. To remain uninvolved, with the hope of converting men to God or even to an acceptance of an ideology of justice, would be to deny the function of the Christian in the world as well as the reality of the historical circumstances. The need for Christian involvement is clear.

Already in the 16th century, when some of the social sciences were practically unknown, Luther wrote the following pertinent words in his Large Catechism:

> God wishes the reputation, good name, and upright character of our neighbor to be taken away or diminished as little as his money and possessions, that every one may stand in his integrity before wife, children, servants, and neighbors.
>
> ....
>
> Therefore this commandment ["Thou shalt not bear false witness against thy neighbor"] is given first of all that *every one shall help his neighbor to secure his rights, and not allow them to be hindered or twisted,* but shall promote and strictly maintain them, no matter whether he be judge or witness, and let it pertain to whatsoever it will. And especially is a goal set up here for our jurists that they be careful to deal truly and uprightly with every case, allowing right to remain right, and, on the other hand, not perverting anything [by their tricks and technical points turning black into white and making wrong out to be right], nor

> glossing it over or keeping silent concerning it, irrespective of a person's money, possession, honor, or power. [1]

In a discussion of "the Biblical authority for the social and political message of the churches today," the Division of Studies of the World Council of Churches proposed the following theses: "It is impossible for the Church adequately to bear witness to the redemptive act of God, which is made manifest to us in the Incarnation, the Passion and Death, and the Resurrection of Jesus Christ, unless *it also makes those pronouncements on human justice which it has a duty to make. . . . What the Church has to say about human law and justice cannot remain isolated and in separation from its proclamation of the crucified, risen, and returning Lord. . . . There is no place for a separated ecclesiastical existence in this world or its States, such as would leave the world or the States to their own devices.* The Church, like the State, is not an end in itself. It exists to bear witness to the plenipotentiary claim of Jesus Christ, and to do so in standing relationship to the existing State." [2]

In the area of social justice a true witness to Jesus Christ cannot stop at speaking good words about God and man and justice. In order that words may be true and effective, they must be accompanied by deeds of love and justice. The speaker of the words must identify himself with people in their need for justice. While this concern is to be demonstrated in every area of life in the world of people, it is imperative that it be expressed in the area of politics, government, and law.

In modern industrialized society, a stable government is a *sine qua non.* And in such a government, especially if it has a democratic structure like that of the United States, the area susceptible to greatest influence in the interest of justice and equity is of course the government itself.

As a result of the several factors contributing to the revolutionary process now going on and affecting the social order throughout the world, governments which are really in control of their nations are taking over more and more control of the lives of their people. This is not merely nor necessarily a greedy reaching out for more power for power's sake but rather a part of the evolution of the revolution itself. And the revolution as well as the centralization of more authority in the state are inevitable unless by some magic happening—or divine intervention—those causes of the revolution (population explosion, industrialization, etc.) suddenly cease to exist. But whether a Christian has a liberal or a conservative political attitude, his interest in justice and equity must be his primary concern as he witnesses to Christ through the exercise of his citizenship responsibility.

Alan Paton calls justice and equity supratemporal goods.[3] They are the stuff of creation and throughout the history of mankind have always been in jeopardy because of the self-centeredness of man in his rebellion against God. The government's responsibility is centered in the temporal needs of people—peace, health, food, housing, economic security, etc. But the supratemporal must always be the concern of the Christian; that is what he must try to help secure and to safeguard also through the medium of the temporal power.

Scruples About Cooperating

There are others too, of course, who have a concern for justice and equity, people of a non-Christian religious persuasion, especially many of our Jewish citizens—and they at times, in their concern for the supratemporal, put many Christians to shame. And some people who make no profession of religious faith but are motivated by enlightened self-interest are stalwart advocates of justice and equity through governmental channels. If, however, the premise set forth in this chapter is correct—that a Christian by virtue of his new life in Baptism is a member of the kingdom of the right hand—then he as a member of the kingdom of the left hand has both the greater potential as well as the greater responsibility to establish and to safeguard, through the medium of government, the supratemporal in the temporal.

As Christians endeavor to carry out this their high calling in Christ, they at times find themselves in a bind. For example: Some whose political thought is more conservative may find it difficult to participate in a concerted civil rights effort with those whose motivations are not Christian. But such scruples are completely unfounded; those who entertain them are ignoring the fact that in other areas of their temporal existence, and to reach less lofty goals than the securing of the supratemporal values called civil rights, they work with people whose motivations are not Christian. In a pluralistic society such as ours in the United States, life in society would be impossible if cooperation with those of various motivations for the attainment of certain common objectives were not a part of the accepted cultural pattern. Even a hermit would be hard put to avoid such cooperation.

Some of the less lofty goals toward which also those of a more conservative mind work in cooperation with society as a whole are to supply their creature wants in labor, industry, business, recreation, entertainment, and a host of other endeavors. But such cooperation is imperative for a Christian, not only to supply his own creaturely or temporal wants, but because, as a new man in Christ, he must be concerned with the proper functioning of society according to the order of creation and God's purpose in it; and he is called upon to do this in cooperation with other men whom God may use to establish and govern a stable and just society.

This then is a source of ongoing tension in the life of a Christian lived out in the kingdom of the left hand: while working with people of other motivations, also earthbound people, the Christian is ever seeking a higher goal—justice and equity for all, *to the glory of God.*

To Obey or Not Is the Problem

The Constitution of the United States, as it has been interpreted by the U. S. Supreme Court—the final arbiter of the Constitution—guarantees justice and equality of opportunity, not to races and ethnic groups, but to citizens regardless of racial or ethnic background. In some parts of our country, in individual towns, cities, or states, there are certain ordinances or in some instances unwritten laws which local authorities consider binding, which deny justice and equal opportunity to some citizens because they are considered members of certain minority racial or ethnic groups. What the Supreme Court says is the constitutional right of all citizens, some local or state laws or customs would deny to certain citizens. Is it right, under such circumstances, to violate the custom or law which contradicts the Federal Constitution as interpreted by the Supreme Court? If it is right to violate such local or state laws, can it be wrong under certain circumstances not to violate them? These are not merely academic questions which may or may not be related to day-by-day life in the United States; they touch the very nerve center of the race issue.

In many places law enforcement agencies are either denying

the Constitution of the United States as interpreted by the Supreme Court, or they are circumventing its enforcement. Orderly demonstrations, however, carried out in keeping with the prerogative afforded citizens by the Constitution of the United States, call attention to the grievances which cause persons to demonstrate and show their concern for removal of the grievances.[4]

In evaluating such demonstrations it becomes necessary in the first place to remember the chain of command that exists in society. It is found operative in all social relations: in the home, in the school, in business, in industry, in government, and in the military. The command of the general takes precedence over that of the sergeant. And the law of the land, the Constitution of the United States as interpreted by the Supreme Court, takes precedence over the command of the police captain who is under the command of a Birmingham police commissioner. Demonstrators respecting the Constitution of the United States may be showing the highest respect for and obedience toward the law by going to jail. They may be saying "yes" to the Constitution but "no" to the local or state law which runs counter to the Constitution. To obey or not to obey may determine one's patriotic loyalty and respect for and acceptance of the rule of law, the authority of Caesar, the divinely ordained temporal power.[5]

But the supratemporal is always of paramount importance; in the final analysis it is the chief concern which the new man in Christ brings with him into the kingdom of the left hand. There is a higher law than the supreme law of the land, namely, the new commandment, the commandment to love one another (John 13:34). Almost in the same breath that St. Paul says, "Let every person be subject to the governing authorities" (Rom. 13:1), he says also, "Owe no man anything, except to love one another; for he who loves his neighbor has fulfilled the Law. . . . Love does no wrong to a neighbor; therefore love is the fulfilling of the Law" (Rom. 13:8, 10). This is the *agape* emphasis of Christ and His most articulate apostle. It demands the surrender by the state and all other worldly authority of any claim to ultimate allegiance on the part of men. There are limits beyond which worldly power cannot go.

Examples of Christ and the Apostles

The relationship of obedience to temporal authority and obedience to Him who both bestows and limits that authority is attested to by the Old Testament prophets,[6] by heroes of the faith, and by Christ Himself.

A classic example of God's sovereignty as expressed in the lives of Christ's apostles is shown when Peter and John stood as prisoners before the Sanhedrin and were charged "not to speak or teach at all in the name of Jesus," and they answered, "Whether it is right in the sight of God to listen to you rather than to God, you must judge; for we cannot but speak of what we have seen and heard" (Acts 4:18-20). When they were brought into court a second time and were told to desist from witnessing to Christ, they replied, "We must obey God rather than men." (Acts 5:29)

A "sit-in" by St. Paul, by which he resisted the civil authorities, is described as follows: "When it was day, the magistrates sent the police, saying, 'Let those men go.' And the jailer reported the words to Paul, saying, 'The magistrates have sent to let you go; now therefore come out and go in peace.' But Paul said to them, 'They have beaten us publicly, uncondemned, men who are Roman citizens, and have thrown us into prison; and do they now cast us out secretly? No! let them come themselves and take us out." (Acts 16:35-37)

But it is Christ, the "last Adam," the one real Man, the express Image and Likeness of God (Col. 1:15), who recognized the temporal authority as well as its limitations, who by word and example teaches us how to regard such authority and how to react to its mandates. The "collectors of the half-shekel tax" asked Peter, "Does not your teacher pay the tax?" Peter answered correctly, "Yes." After the matter was brought to Jesus' attention, He told Peter: "Go to the sea and cast a hook, and take the first fish that comes up, and when you open its mouth you will find a shekel; take that and give it to them for Me and for yourself" (Matt. 17:24-27). He recognized, respected, and obeyed duly constituted governmental authority. He did so not only by paying taxes but also by making the final payment, submitting to death by crucifixion at the hands of civil authorities.

In defense of others, however, Christ challenged and violated both law and custom, putting the supratemporal above the temporal. He broke the Sabbath law by healing the sick on that day. He drove the money changers out of the temple in defiance of the religious-civic authority that had given them license to be there. Although the accusers of the woman taken in adultery had called Jesus' attention to the police law of the Old Testament (Deut. 22:23-24), with divine mercy and compassion toward the woman He said to them: "He that is without sin among you, let him first cast a stone at her." (John 8:3-7 KJV)

Christ clearly distinguished between the temporal and the supratemporal; perhaps the best example of this from His life and teachings can be found in His words, "Render to Caesar the things that are Caesar's, and to God the things that are God's" (Luke 20:25). It is the responsibility of "Caesar" to make justice and equity secure for all citizens. When this function is violated and injustice and inequity prevail with respect to a large segment of society, giving "to God the things that are God's" may impel the Christian not only to say, "We must obey God rather than men" but to translate the word of fidelity to God into action in keeping with the example of Christ.

"It is only in relation to the *regnum mundi* [the kingdom of the world, or the kingdom of the left hand] that the *regnum Christi* [the kingdom of Christ, or the kingdom of the right hand] shows its clarity and power."[7] An *agape*-motivated involvement of Christians in the affairs of men, in government, politics, and law, to strengthen justice and to counteract injustice, even when the doing of it may call for peaceful resistance to the perpetrators of injustice, is evidence of a consistently faithful commitment to the Christ who in the kingdom of grace gives men His new life.

8

Interracial Marriage — Bane or Blessing?

If the Son makes you free, you will be free indeed.

John 8:36

The question, "Would you want your daughter to marry a Negro?" whether asked north or south of the Mason-Dixon line, often stands as a roadblock, making progress in racial understanding all but impossible. Gunnar Myrdal says, "Not only in the South but often also in the North the stereotyped and hypothetical question is regularly raised without any intermediary reasoning as to its application or relevance to the social problem discussed." [1] It matters not what facet of race relations is under discussion—whether it be acceptance of people into the total life and activity of the church; racial justice in the courts of law; equality of opportunity in employment; the use of public facilities; the building, buying, or renting of a house; or federal legislation guaranteeing first-class citizenship—the question of interracial marriage, like Damocles' sword, is always present, ready to cut off rational discussion. Or, to change the metaphor, it is the red herring intended to make reason irrational and logic impossible.

> Let us call this the "re-fencing" device. When a fact cannot fit into a mental field, the exception is acknowledged, but the field is hastily fenced in again and not allowed to remain dangerously open.
>
> A curious instance of re-fencing takes place in many discussions concerning the Negro. When a person with a strong anti-Negro bias is confronted with evidence favorable to the Negro, he frequently pops up with the well-known matrimonial question: "Would you want your sister to marry a Negro?" This re-fencing is adroit. As soon as the interlocutor says, "No," or hesitates in his reply, the biased person can say in effect, "See, there just *is* something different and impossible about the Negro," or, "I was right all along—for the Negro has an objectionable essence in his nature." [2]

Opponents of racial integration are often afraid that some evil will befall them or others if interracial marriage takes place. And so they inject their personal fears into the discussion, and because of their fears they would withhold from others their rights—whether in the church or in society in general.

According to God's purpose, the church and its privileges and responsibilities are intended for all those who answer responsibly to God's gracious call. All other matters are extraneous and for that reason irrelevant—personal fears as to who may marry whom notwithstanding.

A similar principle applies to society outside the confines of the church. The Constitution of the United States as defined by its lawful interpreter, the Supreme Court, guarantees all citizens justice and equal opportunity under the law for "life, liberty, and the pursuit of happiness." To inject the question of interracial marriage into the discussion of constitutional rights is to introduce an irrelevant matter. When the fear of interracial marriage is thus used to curtail the constitutional rights of citizens, the fearful one is using his own emotions unpatriotically against those who are his fellow citizens and against the "due process of law."

There are a number of things that the person beset by the fear of interracial marriage can do. He can seek a different homeland, and unless he goes to the Republic of South Africa, his fears will perhaps grow into a haunting obsession by day and by night; he will be jumping out of the interracial-marriage frying pan into the consuming fire of his fear-ridden self. The best that can be done for the person whose fears are expressed in the interracial marriage question is to counsel him to give up the dog-in-the-manger act and to quit barking at those who would enjoy the good provender supplied them by the Creator: the right to live as God's human creatures, restored to sonship through His grace and living in God's good world where, according to His purpose, justice and equity are of its very essence. The fearful one crying out against interracial marriage could be counseled to ask himself why he is doing so, and it could be suggested that he eliminate his opposition rather than try to withhold the free use of the good things of creation from someone else.

What the Scriptures Say

Although the Scriptures are all but silent on the question of interracial marriage, their answer to the question as it is thrown into the arena of the current race issue by the segregationist is unmistakably clear.

The Scriptures are very clear in their testimony to the oneness of the human family, and modern science substantiates such oneness. This unity of the human family did not vanish as soon as it was created. Our first parents, created by God, became the parents of offspring through a power the Creator gave them, the power of procreation. As God, then, established the unity of the human family in creation, He continued this family unity through procreation, that is, the power to reproduce through the act of sex.

God is operative in procreation and through natural processes is creating people all the time. He creates the "white" man, and He creates the "yellow" man and the "black" man. Must we assume, though, that in some way He has withdrawn His creative power, to make of some a sort of self-propagating robot altogether detached from the mind, the will, the power, and the purpose of God when they procreate the untold millions, the great majority of those dwelling on earth today, who are neither "black" nor "white" nor "yellow"?

The segregationist who on either biological or moral grounds would try to deprecate interracial marriage, in doing so—although possibly unwittingly—is blaspheming the Creator God. "He Himself gives to all men life and breath and everything" (Acts 17:25), and "in Him we live and move and have our being" (Acts 17:28). In witnessing to God through Christ, the attack against the Bible-quoting segregationist must be at the Achilles' heel, seemingly the only place of vulnerability: "By your anti-interracial-marriage propaganda you are blaspheming the God of *all* creation whose honor you purportedly would defend. You are desecrating that which God has consecrated—man." Or, in a more evangelical spirit and in recognition of the guilt in which all Americans are involved in one way or another, would it be helpful to paraphrase St. Paul?

> To My White Brethren in the Churches of America:
>
> Grace be to you and peace from God the Father, and from our Lord Jesus Christ, Who gave Himself for our sins, that He might deliver us from this evil world according to the will of God, our Father; to whom be glory for ever and ever. Amen.
>
> I write to you concerning the Negro, whom God hath made to differ from us in color only, but whom we have rejected as a lesser creature, *committing thereby a grievous sin against the impartial Creator.*
>
> I write not to judge, but to urge repentance, and deeds born of repentance.[3]

Interracial Marriage in the Old Testament

Following are a few examples of Old Testament intermarriage

prohibitions: Deut. 7:1-3; Joshua 23:3-13; Ezra 9:12; 10:10-11; Neh. 10:30; 13:23-31. In none of the passages so often quoted in favor of segregation and against interracial marriage is race involved as we understand the term today. The prohibition is always on religious or moral grounds.

There is an instance of what seems to be a truly interracial marriage spoken of in the Old Testament which the segregationists do not adduce. In this case it is God Himself, not one of His human spokesmen, who disapproves. But His disapproval is not of the marriage but of those who criticized the marriage. Miriam, the sister of Moses, and Aaron, his brother, spoke against Moses because he, a Hebrew, had married a Cushite woman. Then God took the matter in hand. In punishment Miriam was smitten with leprosy. (See Num. 12.)

The story is a clear revelation of the attitude of God toward interracial marriage. According to the text, He neither favors nor disfavors it; rather, He ignores that which is the center of our present concern. And in doing so He declares the whole matter quite irrelevant to His purpose of communicating with His people and ruling in their lives. But while it seems that Miriam and Aaron wanted to make the issue of race an integral part of the theocratic governmental structure that God was creating, God, without addressing Himself to the self-evident unity of the human family that He had created, condemned the segregationists, Miriam and Aaron. They were interfering in His business, as the modern segregationists would do through their question, "Would you want your daughter to . . .?" or with such questions as: "Would you want Negroes to vote and soon to rule? Would you want Negro children to go to school with your children? Would you want to go to Holy Communion with Negroes? Would you want to live next door to a Negro?"

The Creator, who is also the divine Judge with power to impose on the disobedient a far worse sentence than a few days of unpleasant leprosy, will have nothing of segregationist piety—neither of the Aaron and Miriam type nor of the modern anti-interracial-marriage variety.

The Old Testament presents a history of God's dealing with Abraham the Hebrew and his descendants called Hebrews, later called the Children of Israel. Any intermarriage discussed in the Old Testament must be understood in this context: marriage between Hebrew and Hebrew, and marriage between Hebrew and non-Hebrew. Segregationists try to establish Biblical authority for their strictures against interracial marriage by quoting Bible passages which under certain circumstances forbade or condemned marriage of Hebrews to non-Hebrews. But in the same Old Testament writings numerous cases of Hebrew-non-Hebrew marriages are recorded but not condemned. (Gen. 38:2; 41:50; Ex. 2:21)

Lev. 24:10-23 is a passage that may shed light on the discussion. The Israelites were then on the wilderness journey. An Israelite (Hebrew) woman had a son by an Egyptian man, probably her husband. Her son "blasphemed the Name." Because of his blasphemy, according to an oracle received by Moses from God, the son of the Israelite woman was stoned to death. According to many scholars, the Egyptians were a Negroid people. But whether the Egyptian father was Negroid or not, the racial background of the son had nothing whatever to do with his condemnation and consequent execution; rather, he was condemned and stoned for religious or spiritual reasons: because he had "blasphemed the Name." Here again, though the intermarriage (or miscegenation) aspect of the story is mentioned, it is altogether irrelevant to the pronouncement of guilty or not guilty.

The Old Testament record, besides referring to specific Hebrew-non-Hebrew marriages, in some places also reveals that this type of mixed marriage, or miscegenation within the same type of ethnic stock, was very prevalent among the Israelites. In Ex. 12:38 one reads that a "mixed multitude" went up with the Israelites on their journey out of Egypt. Num. 11:4 (KJV) again refers to "the mixed multitude" that was among them. And Num. 31:9 records that Israel "took captive the women of Midian and their little ones," while the Midianite men were destroyed; and Deut. 21:10-13 makes legal provision for the marriage of non-Hebrews to Hebrews.

Christ a "Mongrel"

The Bible tells us that many of the great Hebrew men of God were either married to non-Hebrew spouses or were the offspring of such unions; e. g., Joseph, Moses, David, and Solomon. The most devastating witness against the Bible-quoting advocates of racial purity is the person whom the segregationists claim to be serving—the Lord Jesus Christ. In the genealogies found in the New

Testament writings Christ is presented as a descendant of David, and in many New Testament passages David is referred to as an ancestor of Christ. But David was not of "pure Hebrew blood." His great-grandmother, Ruth, was a Moabite woman. Rahab, the Canaanite harlot who received the two spies sent into the land by Joshua and hid them under the flax laid out upon the housetop (Joshua 2:1-21), was a maternal ancestor of Jesus.

Even if whiteness were an evidence of racial superiority, white supremacists could not lay claim to whiteness as though it were the result of their own accomplishment. In fact, they had nothing to do with it; it all happened when they were conceived in their mother's womb. What about Christ, whose ancestor, David, had a Moabite great-grandmother? What about Christ, who had among His ancestors the Canaanite *harlot* Rahab? Did He have anything to do with what He was according to human ancestry? He did. He chose to be a descendant of both Ruth, the Moabite woman, and Rahab, the Canaanite harlot. For He is God incarnate, the God of history, also of the history of His human ancestry. What a blow to the segregationist who would maintain his racial superiority by fighting against interracial marriage! For Christ is the descendant of a mixed (Hebrew and non-Hebrew) union, and according to God's redemptive purpose one of His ancestors was a harlot. If the segregationist wants above all to be identified with Christ, he must, within the oneness of the human family in which Christ can be found, give up his claim of white superiority and his fight against the God-ordained institution of holy matrimony blessed through a sign at the wedding feast at Cana by the Descendant of Rahab and Ruth.

If the question of interracial marriage has in it the implication that on the other side of the racial fence there is more sin—the sin of loose sex life and concomitant social disease—then the questioner in his stereotyping is condemning many chaste and innocent people. But what is of even greater moment, in moral prudishness he is also denying the Christ who "came to seek and to save the lost" (Luke 19:10) and in doing so could call all men His fellows (Heb. 2:11), also the harlot Rahab. That is the humility of Christ, and that is the humility required of those who would be the followers of Christ.

To Advocate or Not

But—"Would you *advocate* interracial marriage?"

Not to advocate interracial marriage is not necessarily to deny its validity. Interracial marriage is valid whether it is advocated or not. But the overwhelming number of those who recognize and emphasize the validity of interracial marriage—contrary to the interpretation of their stance by some of the advocates of segregation—do not advocate such marriages. This is especially true of Negroes. Gunnar Myrdal discusses "the white man's rank order of discriminations. . . . Highest in this order stands the bar against intermarriage and sexual intercourse involving white women." Lowest in rank "come the discriminations in securing land, credit, jobs, or other means of earning a living, and discriminations in public relief and other social welfare activities." Myrdal states that "the Negro's own rank order is just about parallel, but inverse, to that of the white man." Contrary to popular thought when Myrdal made his study—the popular thought when this book was written—"the Negro resists least the discrimination on the ranks placed highest in the white man's evaluation and resents most any discrimination on the lowest level." [4]

Although the great majority of those who accept the validity of interracial marriage do not advocate it, there are logical and moral arguments that advocates of interracial marriage can present and to which a thoughtful and socially concerned Christian will want to listen. For example—and this is perhaps an oversimplification—racial prejudice and racial discrimination, of which racial segregation is a tool, is present in our society because there are within our society certain racial groups against whom racial prejudice and discrimination can be directed and whose members can be segregated. If there were no identifiable racial groups, then racial prejudice, discrimination, and segregation could not exist.

While the changing of man's environment will not of itself change the prejudiced nature of man, it can affect racial prejudice, discrimination, and segregation; it can cause them to increase or decrease and, with respect to certain identifiable racial traits, eliminate them altogether. With the latter in mind—and under the restrictions which Christian love always places upon us (however it may be expressed in certain circumstances)—would it be wrong in any sense to advocate interracial marriage?

There is untold suffering in the world and in our society today because evil, selfish men have exploited the distinctive physical traits which God has given to men to make them human. Would it be wrong, then, to advocate that which in its consummation would make racial exploitation impossible? Other forms of exploitation would arise in a "raceless" human society but their inevitability should not hinder the elimination of one that is now plaguing us. If it were wrong to eliminate the environmental factor—identifiable racial traits—because exploitation of another kind will arise out of a new environment, it would be equally wrong to educate men, because such education can become, as it often does, potentially exploitable; thus every form of social reform would be wrong. The seasoned preacher knows too well that the sermon he is to deliver on the following Sunday will not eradicate sin altogether from the lives of his listeners, but he continues to preach against sin Sunday after Sunday and year after year.

In our society, in which the number of those who actually advocate intermarriage is infinitesimally small—the writer bespeaks its validity but is not an advocate of it—there are millions of people who are now suffering unjustly simply because they were born with the genes that make it impossible for them to be classified as white. That is the lot of most racial minority groups in our society, and our 20 million Negroes experience it most. Negroes suffer unjustly, and their children will, until racial discrimination is eliminated from our society; the husband and wife in an interracial marriage suffer unjustly, and their children will also. That is a plain sociological phenomenon that cannot be denied and is one of the chief reasons for these many words on interracial marriage.

Can right-thinking people, then, censure those who for good reasons want to change the status quo by advocating interracial marriage? There is a German proverb to the effect that shared sorrow divides sorrow. And there is another "proverb" which St. Paul addresses to those who are members of the body of Christ: "Rejoice with those who rejoice; weep with those who weep" (Rom. 12:15). More important, he tells them: "Bear one another's burdens and so fulfill the law of Christ." (Gal. 6:2)

The idea is prevalent in our society—perhaps too prevalent also among many Christians—that romantic love is the one necessary ingredient of marital success and bliss. "As long as they truly love each other, nothing else matters much." But romantic love, in itself a gift of God, is but a sex-induced emotion which, if it stands alone, can be of little value in sustaining a marriage and making it truly successful. The mutually shared love of God in Christ (Eph. 5:21-33) and the abiding presence of the Spirit of God are of greater value and importance to the marital couple than romantic love standing alone.

But there is another essential ingredient for a successful and blissful marriage: a degree of common interest and ideals. For man's life is not intended merely for his own sake, that he may be happy, content, secure. God and fellowman must somehow be found in the scheme of man's life. The vertical and the horizontal are always important—man's relation to God and man's relation to his fellowman—the well-being of one's fellowman and the glory of God. But while the glory of God is the final purpose of all creation, the well-being of one's fellowman must at all times be fostered; and that is a means of glorifying God. It is at this point in the God-man relationship and the man-man relationship that mutual interests and worthy ideals fit into the picture of a God-pleasing marriage.

God does not give all of His people the same insight and understanding of their fellowman's needs, nor does He give all of them the same strength and courage to help meet those needs. It is conceivable, nevertheless, that some young people may be gifted by God with ideals and mutual interests that would make them sufficiently far-visioned to want to help change our social environment so that racial discrimination and its most effective weapon, racial segregation, would be made impossible—and having such an ideal as a part of their life's blueprint would commit themselves to holy interracial marriage. If they are asked, "What about your children?" they could respond, "We do not want to shield our children selfishly from the burden that our present social environment places into the laps of millions of children who, because they are of Negro or other racial minority parentage, are doomed to lifelong, shameful discrimination. We shall, God helping us, with a higher goal than merely selfishly protecting ourselves and our children from hurt, assume our responsibility to share in that burden of hurt to help change our environment until it is impossible to hurt anyone because of his racial identity." There are people who, unlike the rest of us, consider advocating and participating in interracial marriage a worthy ideal and a goal toward which to strive. On the basis of Christian social concern it would be hard to gainsay their purposes. One marriage counselor writes:

> I can see no final end to racial prejudice and no final solution to interracial problems until marriage between black and white or red and yellow is as acceptable as marriages today between blonds and brunets or brunets and redheads. Could it not be that among the mature and courageous Christian young men and women of our land there would be those who, enlightened and strengthened by the Spirit of God, could take the lead in this tremendous battle for the rights and the freedom of all mankind? Interracial marriage is not a problem; it is a challenge.[5]

A different approach. Some white couples are developing interracial families by adopting nonwhite children. Ex-GI's, especially after the Korean conflict, adopted Korean orphans; and now a number of clergymen and their spouses, as well as others, in California, Illinois, Indiana, Iowa, Ohio, and Minnesota, have adopted Negro and Indian orphans. Parents to Adopt Minority Youngsters (PAMY), operating out of St. Paul, Minn., is organized for the purpose of recruiting adoptive parents and has as one of its chief goals the securing of white homes for nonwhite children. Nineteen religious and social welfare agencies are sponsors of PAMY.

Miscegenation Outside of Marriage—an Abomination

The world and the church are not served well by trying to maintain in society the doubtful status quo implicit in the question, "Would you want your daughter to marry a Negro?" As the builder of a new society the Christian has a more constructive role to play. He may not have the insight, courage, and conviction that would necessarily make of him an advocate of interracial marriage. But one thing must be clear: any social system which in its very nature is conducive to miscegenation outside the bonds of matrimony—and that is the nature of our present social system as it has developed—must be condemned and resisted. Especially where anti-interracial-marriage laws have been on the statute books and the power structure of the community has given little or no protection to Negro women, the grossest of sex crimes have been and still are being committed against members of the minority group.[6]

A Southerner, a member of the House of Representatives, admits the following:

> Bereft of any real protection from their own men and denied (until recently) any measure of legal protection, Negro women have been victimized by white masters and white men for generations. The lasting and visible proof of this is the presence in our midst of considerable numbers of Negroes of mixed blood. A number of anthropologists, among them Professor Melville J. Herskovits and Alex Hrdlicka, report surveys which show that as many as 70 out of 100 Negroes can lay claim to one or more white ancestors.
>
> That astoundingly high ratio seems due primarily to the incidence of concubinage during slavery days, when extra-legal sex relations with slave women on the part of slave-owners and/or their sons was tolerated, although not applauded. The birth of every mulatto child of such a union tended to accelerate the diffusion of white blood into the Negro race, since the fate of the mulatto in this country always has been to be forced into the lower rather than the higher level of parentage.[7]

A Harlem pastor, Clemonce Sabourin, who spent more than half of his life in states which had anti-interracial-marriage laws, says:

> These laws have declared open season on Negro women. For white men who go with Negro women are not only not forced to, they are actually not permitted to, shoulder the responsibility for their acts. But the white woman has protection. If a white man goes with her, he has to shoulder the responsibility. If a Negro goes with her, and is caught, it's a sad, sordid story. Negro pastors who have witnessed it, report that even today in certain places, because of fear and intimidation, Negroes have little authority over their own chastity. This is not intermarriage, which is honorable in all. This is the immorality and adultery that God condemns.[8]

The popularity of extramarital miscegenation, especially in the South, is a fact that cannot be gainsaid. "Segregation in the South has always been what proud Negroes bitterly, and proud whites jovially, call 'day-time segregation,'"[9] an overt expression of the innate selfishness of fallen man.

Applying the Balm

When the truth is accepted that interracial marriage is in itself legitimate from a theological viewpoint, what then? This is the question which confronts every Christian conscience. "What are you doing in word, deed, and association to help racially mixed couples . . . to strengthen their partnership, to be received by their environment, to have all possible assistance in bringing up their children?" [10]

If and when interracial marriage takes place, the well-being of the couple as well as their children becomes the concern of all, beginning with the families involved and then radiating to wider and ever wider circles. Whether the marriage ceremony is performed by a justice of the peace or the couple is united by the church in holy wedlock, with pastor and congregation invoking the blessing of God upon them, the church must become God's agent to bring into their lives the blessing of God—in this instance Christian fellowship and all that the term involves: full acceptance and identification with the couple. "What therefore God has joined together, let not man put asunder" (Mark 10:9) is not mere theological abstraction or at most a serious warning to husband and wife to do everything possible to maintain their marriage; it involves others too. All are to lend their aid, and the responsibility of the Christian is greatest because he has received the special blessing of the new life of God, the life of love in Christ.

Among the many opportunities that a Christian has to translate faith into action, the one afforded him when an interracial couple needs his cooperation and help is not to be considered unimportant. When the couple is in need of acceptance and friendship, many of the Christian virtues can and must be expressed. The whole of the new life of the baptized believer is then called into action. He is called upon to live dangerously, for by accepting those whom society rejects, he himself may be rejected. By challenging the status quo which opposes interracial marriage, he in turn is challenged to live out his Christian life.

We are confronted with the stark fact that "more often than not, when a person marries outside his own race, there are members of his own family who will disown him; his friends avoid him; his colleagues ignore him; his employer fires him; his landlord evicts him; his own fellow citizens in enlightened, Christian America persecute him; and this in spite of the fact that marriage is honorable in all." [11]

In such an atmosphere of hatred the Christian is called upon to love. Promised ease and security by ignoring those whom society ignores, but instead identifying himself with them, he may be inviting death in more than one way. That is the nature of the Christian life at every turn; that is its nature also when the Christian is called upon to help human beings struggling under the burden that an unfriendly, selfish society places upon the shoulders of those who in marriage cross over the tightly drawn racial line.

A Matter of Interpretation

The devil can appear as an angel of light, and his "goodness" and "virtue" are seemingly never more obvious than when he tries to speak theologically—as God's good interpreter—or when he quotes Bible passages. This is especially true of the matter under discussion in this book and specifically in this chapter on interracial marriage.

The Genesis story of the fall into sin finds the devil asking Eve, "Did God say, 'You shall not eat of any tree of the garden'?" When Eve had quoted God to this effect, "You shall not eat of the fruit of the tree which is in the midst of the garden, neither shall you touch it, lest you die," Satan responded: "You will not die. For God knows that when you eat of it your eyes will be opened and you will be like God, knowing good and evil." (Gen. 3:1-5)

When Jesus, by the Spirit's guidance, was led into the wilderness, Satan tried to put on a pious front by reminding Him of what had happened at His baptism; His Father had said, "This is My beloved Son, with whom I am well pleased" (Matt. 3:17). Satan said, "*If You are the Son of God,* command these stones to become loaves of bread." When Jesus did not comply, Satan tried again, not only donning a facade of piety but assuming the appearance of authority. He quoted the written record: "If You are the Son of God, throw Yourself down, for it is written, 'He will give His angels charge of you,' and 'On their hands they will bear you up, lest you strike your foot against a stone.'" Meeting Satan at his own game, Jesus quoted from the Scriptures and did it successfully, answering to the first temptation, "It is written, 'Man shall not live by bread alone, but by every word that proceeds from the mouth of God.'" To the second temptation He replied, "Again it is written, 'You shall not tempt the Lord your God.'" And after the third temptation, Jesus said not only "Begone, Satan!" but also "for it is written, 'You shall worship the

Lord your God, and Him only shall you serve.'" (Matt. 4:1-10)

It is even so today. Satan and sometimes some Christians quote the Scriptures erroneously; and Christ, through His Spirit dwelling in man, quotes the Scriptures. How can the voice of Satan be distinguished from the call of the Spirit of God as men quote the Scriptures in support of a position which favors or opposes racial segregation?

Adding answer to answer is not the answer. People need more than answers to find their way through a labyrinth of conflicting ideas about race. What they need is faith, faith in the Christ who is "the Way and the Truth and the Life" (John 14:6). To those who were looking for more and better answers from the Scriptures, Jesus, who is Himself the Answer, responded: "You search the Scriptures because you think that in them you have eternal life; and it is they that bear witness to Me." (John 5:39)

What is God's ultimate purpose in all His acts to which the Scriptures testify? Where shall we find answers to the many facets of God's relation to man, man's relation to God, and man's relation to man? The criterion of all truly Biblical doctrine and answers is the one Answer, Jesus Christ.

9

The Church and Its Function

. . . one holy, catholic and apostolic church.
The Nicene Creed

The Church Is People

The word "church" as it is used in the Greek New Testament means people, specific people restored to manhood and in a certain relationship to God and their fellowmen. When the word "church," then, is used in its Biblical meaning, the discussion is always about people; for example, "You are . . . God's own *people*" (1 Peter 2:9); "He says in Hosea, 'Those who were not *My people* I will call "My people"'" (Rom. 9:25); "God said . . . 'I will be their God, and they shall be *My people*'" (2 Cor. 6:16). Christ "gave Himself for us to redeem us from all iniquity and to purify for Himself *a people* of His own who are zealous for good deeds" (Titus 2:14). The church is important because it is people; and people are important.

While it is true that the church is "called-out" people *(ecclesia)*, the word itself does not mean people, but rather an assembly of people. More specifically, the church is an assembly of people who in faith and confidence call Jesus Lord (1 Cor. 12:3) and also assemble in the name of the Lord. Almost every conceivable assembly of believers in the New Testament is called the church.

Jesus said where "two or three" assembled in His name He would be in their midst. By assembling in His name they become the church (Matt. 18:17-20). The Christian household is spoken of as the church; examples: the church in the home of Prisca and Aquila (Rom. 16:3, 5; 1 Cor. 16:19); the church in the house of Nympha (Col. 4:15); and the church in the house of Philemon (Philemon 2). The term "church" is also applied in the New Testament to what today is called a congregation or parish, for example, the church at Cenchreae (Rom. 16:1), the church at Corinth (1 Cor. 1:2 and 2 Cor. 1:1), the church at Thessalonica (1 Thess. 1:1), and the church of the Laodiceans. (Col. 4:16)

Perhaps the most important New Testament use of the term "church" is when it is employed to signify the sum total of all people in the world who in faith and trust confess that "Jesus Christ is Lord," for example: "Christ loved the church and gave Himself up for her" (Eph. 5:25). It is this use of the word "church" that we find in older versions of two of the ecumenical creeds: in the Apostles' Creed, "I believe in the holy catholic [universal, Christian] church"; in the Nicene Creed, "I believe in one holy, catholic [universal, Christian], and apostolic church."

You Can See *the Church*

This universal church in which all believers are through Christ united with God and with their fellow believers in a family relationship is to be *seen* wherever the church is found: in the assembly of "two or three" gathered in Jesus' name, in the Christian household, in the local congregation, as well as in larger assemblies of Christians. Since people in the church are personalities with a visible, physical anatomy—not disembodied "souls"—the church is always visible. The faith by which they live is indeed invisible, but they themselves are not. It may be true that in given circumstances some who do not believe may assemble with the believers, but the believers themselves (who constitute the church), as long as they are "in the flesh," are altogether visible.

The visibility of the church is emphasized in this connection because of the responsibility—stressed in many places in this book—of Christians to identify themselves with the total need of the total man, whether he is a fellow Christian or not.

Christ prayed for the spiritual unity of His followers, "that they may all be one." But He added, "so that the world may believe that Thou hast sent Me" (John 17:21). The only way by which "the world" of people may know that God has sent Jesus into the world is by the oneness of His followers, who are people quite visible to the eye whenever they are around. This unity of the church is a living force, not an abstract idea. That the human species once broken through sin has now been healed by Christ must be evident in the lives of men through the fellowship of love which they practice, so that other men might be attracted to that fellowship and be healed themselves. Racial segregation and all its unsocial, unloving concomitants, especially when they are found in the church or advocated and supported by church people, vitiate the inward spiritual unity by which the Spirit would unite all men in Christ.[1]

The Church a Sharing Community

The church is more than a visible assembly of people who through Christ are in a new relationship to God and to people. The church is a community of people, that is, a people in communion with God and people. They receive all the blessings of God through Christ, and as they live out their new God-given life there is a continual sharing of these blessings with each other and with people in general (1 John 1:3; Phil. 2:1-11; John 13:34; Rom. 12:16). While this responsibility of sharing embraces the needs of all men, the responsibility of concern is first for those who are a part of the Christian fellowship. (Gal. 6:10)

> Christian is bound to brother Christian, whether he be kinsman or friend or church member, by the ties of love. This means that he assumes responsibility for the spiritual life, as well as physical, of the other. The stronger his own life of the Spirit is, the more painstakingly and sensitively he goes about the task of cherishing the welfare and seeking the good of the brother. Between the people who are already disciples of Christ the operations of Christian love come into their fullest flower.[2]

The primitive church in Jerusalem, shortly after the first Christian Pentecost, seems to have grasped and accepted the sharing nature of Christianity as expressed in a sharing church. They seem to have taken seriously the new commandment given them by Christ, "Love one another," as they established a Christian communal society (Acts 4:32-37). Even though the system was not long-lived, it no doubt was an evident expression of the sharing responsibility inherent in the nature of the church.

A high point of the sharing aspect of the life of the church is found in Holy Communion. All the elements of God's good purpose in creation are to be found in the Holy Supper: God gives Himself to man, man gives himself to God, man eats and drinks with his fellowman in the communion of God's family, and God is praised.

The sons of men become the sons of God through the Sacrament of Holy Baptism; the new Adam, Christ, takes the place of the old Adam, self. Man can now walk in newness of life (Rom. 6:3-11). This new life given by God to man in Baptism is sustained in the Holy Supper of the Lord. In the church, the assembly of God's people, God in Christ gives Himself to His people for victorious living. A post-Communion prayer of the faithful expresses this thought: "O Thou blessed Savior Jesus Christ, *who hast given Thyself to me* in this holy Sacrament, keep me in Thy faith and favor; *as Thou livest in me, let me also live in Thee*." This sharing of His own self—His life, the life of the incarnate Son of God—with His baptized children is expressed in the words of institution of His Supper: "'Take, eat; this is My body.' And He took a cup, and when He had given thanks He gave it to them, saying, 'Drink of it, all of you; for this is My blood of the covenant which is poured out for many for the forgiveness of sins'" (Matt. 26:26-28). That is sharing at its highest level: God in Christ giving Himself to man so that man might live in Him.

The sharing goes both ways, from God to man and from man to God. As man receives the life of God from God, He then gives it back to God as a "living sacrifice," a "spiritual worship" (Rom. 12:1). This worship process has its starting point in the Communion itself, which is called the Holy Eucharist, the feast of thanksgiving. The celebration is surrounded by expressions of the thanksgiving and praise of the communicants, in words spoken and hymns sung by them and in their name by the celebrant. As they partake of the heavenly food, they give their newly received life back to the God from whom they received it.

In the Service of Holy Communion the faithful receive and give in communion, not in isolation from each other. Here the unity of those brought together in God through Christ has its highest expression (1 Cor. 10:16-17). Man separated from man through sin is once again united with his fellowman; the ugly breach is closed; the family is restored. They eat together and—as symbolized especially in the ancient tradition of the use of the common cup—they drink together.

The purpose of the Holy Communion is not limited to the sharing that takes place in the house of God and at the Communion table. What happens then is also symbolical of what, according to the will of God, is to happen outside the walls of the church and the assembly of believers. Renewed in faith and life through Holy Communion, strengthened for the ongoing privilege of witnessing to Christ, the Christian is to go out and to become a part of the lifestream of the secular community, to thank and praise God by sharing with his fellowman the good things that he himself has received from God. "Once a community has accepted a redemptive faith, the impact of their environment upon them forces them either to narrow their concept of redemption by giving it an otherworldly interpretation, or to widen its reference so as to include the whole of their environment." [3]

In Holy Communion, then, God gives; His people first receive, and then in thanksgiving, adoration, and praise to God accept each other and go out from His blessed presence to share with others all the good things He has prepared for man. The Holy Communion is a miniature prototype of creation as intended by God.

The Church as the Body of Christ

The concept of the church as the body of Christ suggests another high point of the sharing aspect of the church's life. The church is the body of Christ; the individual believers are members of the body of which Christ Himself is the Head. Although some interpreters consider this metaphorical language, St. Paul seems to present the thought of the church as the body of Christ as reality rather than a mere figure of speech: "*You are the body of Christ* and individually members of it" (1 Cor. 12:27); "He has put all things under His feet and has made Him the Head over all things for the church, *which is His body,* the fulness of Him who fills all in all." (Eph. 1:22-23; see also Eph. 5:23; Col. 1:18, 24)

In His sacerdotal prayer Christ used similar language: "The glory which Thou hast given Me I have given to them, that they may be one even as We are one, *I in them and Thou in Me,* that they may become perfectly one, so that the world may know that Thou hast sent Me and hast loved them even as Thou hast loved Me" (John 17:22-23). A similar thought is suggested by the last words, as recorded by St. Matthew, which Christ spoke to His disciples immediately before His ascension: "*I am with you always,* to the close of the age." (Matt. 28:20)

But whether the concept of the church as the body of Christ, with Christ Himself as the Head, is interpreted metaphorically or literally, it has the same theological purpose: the church is people who are guided by Christ the Head; He gives them His Spirit to share with one another. In his classic description of the church in 1 Corinthians 12, St. Paul makes this abundantly clear.

The Church Always a Togetherness

What is the church then? Whether it is described as people assembled to glorify God, or as a community in which people receive from God and share with one another, or as the body of Christ with Christ as its Head, the church is always a togetherness, never a separation; and segregation therefore is the direct opposite of what the church is. It cannot be tolerated in the church nor outside of it, because those who are still outside the assembly are to be brought inside.

When the church, then, functions as church, it always functions in and for the unity that is to be found in a healthy, functioning body—in this instance, the body of Christ. St. Paul exhorts the Christians at Ephesus:

> I therefore, a prisoner for the Lord, beg you to lead a life worthy of the calling to which you have been called, with all lowliness and meekness, with patience, forbearing one another in love, eager to maintain the unity of the Spirit in the bond of peace. There is one body and one Spirit, just as you were called to the one hope that belongs to your call, one Lord, one faith, one Baptism, one God and Father of us all, who is above all and through all and in all. (Eph. 4:1-6)

It is the very nature of the church to work in unity with people, not in disunity. When confronted with the separation of South African apartheid or U.S. segregation (Northern or Southern style), the church has the God-given opportunity to show the loving mind of Christ and to demonstrate the essential unity of the human race. It ignores this opportunity at its own peril.

A Few Do's and Don'ts

If the church is people who make up a sharing community united in one body by one Spirit, serving one Lord, and if all people are to be drawn into the sharing fellowship of the church, then a congregation must work at establishing and strengthening its fellowship.

Walls of opposition to the church's God-intended fellowship often confront congregations, especially in the changing communities of our big cities. They are invisible, psychological walls, sometimes of double thickness. They are built in the minds of people of the community surrounding the church and in the minds of members of the congregation itself. Both walls have to be broken down before those who are members of the congregation and those who are not can meet in fellowship and acceptance within the church walls of brick, stone, and mortar. When the church resists or procrastinates in accepting newly arrived nonwhite people of the community, the members themselves will begin to excuse or to rationalize their obvious disobedience to Him who says: "Come unto Me, all ye . . ." (Matt. 11:28); "My house shall be called a house of prayer for all peoples" (Is. 56:7). At the same time the newcomers, observing or sensing the congregation's unwillingness to accept them into the fellowship of the church, will build up their own walls of resistance to the invitation and welcome that comes through so belatedly.

What can be done about these walls? See to it that they are never erected? That is easy to say, and yet it must be said. To avoid the chagrin, embarrassment, and disrepute into which the church will be drawn by a spirit of exclusiveness or aloofness, the invitation and the welcome must be a part of the congregation's way of life—not to be manufactured when there is imminent danger of the collapse of the institutional structure nor when nonwhites first make their appearance in the community.

Having its origin in the Word and the sacraments, this way of life must be a living reality throughout the church's existence. To avoid the problem, its presence must be anticipated before it comes to the surface. How often have pastors and other leaders in the church said of their congregations, "We do not have a race problem"! Though the statement may be made in blissful ignorance, it nevertheless ignores the ever-present threat of the old man of sinful self-centeredness expressing himself in the lives of church members as they, like others, move about in a society saturated with racial prejudice and discrimination.

There are a number of things that a congregation can do to avoid building these hideous, invisible walls.

It must keep working its theology: keep on working with the Word of God in the midst of the congregation. The fundamental catechism truths are not to be neglected. But their mere rehashing, perhaps in the same terminology used by our forefathers, is not enough. The old truths must take on new life as they are applied to the world of today. For example, the truth expressed in the commandment "Thou shalt not steal" becomes alive and challenges the conscience when racial discrimination is described in terms of robbing people of the right to have a decent house, to have an education in keeping with the needs of a modern technological era, or to secure a job adequate for the needs of modern life.

RELEVANT PREACHING

The commandment of God "Thou shalt not kill," known from childhood, begins to function as the word of divine judgment when it is properly applied by the preacher to modern man. What the preacher says will sound like thunder and lightning from Mount Sinai when he tells his hearers that "without malice aforethought" people of gentility take part in the mass murder of millions of our nonwhite fellow citizens, murdering them with the sharp sword of stereotype: "Negroes are a happy, carefree people"; "they are deeply spiritual"; "they are good singers"; "they have an innate sense of rhythm"; or "they are not capable of any high degree of learning, but they have a natural capacity for hard work." The preacher will perform his function as a modern prophet of God when he tells his people that we murder our brothers when we say of Negroes that they are "lazy, immoral, diseased, and once removed from savagery." The preacher will be preaching relevantly to our times when he tells his people that by the use of such stereotypes they deny the humanity of the Negro—a denial that can be as deadly as gun or sword.

It is the function of the prophet "to pluck up and to break down, to destroy and to overthrow" (Jer. 1:10a) by the preaching of a relevant word of divine judgment. It is his further high prerogative "to build and to plant" (Jer. 1:10b). The preacher of the Word is a messenger commissioned to proclaim the mercy of God. His is the exalted calling to make known to and remind his people of the new life that is theirs in Jesus Christ, which makes of them God's people who themselves are to pluck up and break down and overthrow devil-inspired stereotypes and to build and plant a society "alive to all that is good" (1 Peter 2:24 Phillips), where fellowship, justice, and equity are the hallmarks of a new society of men.

Since education, at least in this field, has as its goal motivation to action, the pastor's attitude must be made crystal clear from the very beginning: He is unequivocally opposed to segregation in the church and is committed to a program of complete integration. He is opposed to the one and approves of the other not because he was born in Maine and studied in New York City but because his understanding of and obedience toward the Gospel of salvation has worked this conviction in his heart. His attitude is simply one of humble submission to the Word and will of Christ his Lord.

In making his attitude known to the congregation, the pastor will couch his words in evangelical language; at the throne of God he will seek a spirit of humility; he will endeavor to radiate love toward those who may not yet understand; he will try to be tactful and not stand in the way of the Spirit of God. But in all he says and does, his purpose will be to make his attitude *known,* not to hide it. The honor of Christ is at stake. The pastor will not vacillate. His attitude is the Christ-wrought attitude that must be known and clearly understood by all.

Also in this aspect of his ministry he cannot be a blind leader of the blind. He must have vision if others are to follow him. His members know this. For this reason they have called him to be their shepherd. When a degree of rapport has been established, the congregation normally expects the pastor to take a stand on vital issues to which God has spoken. For this reason they come week after week to hear him. Yes, in a sense they have entrusted their spiritual care into his hands. Though Christ is the great Shepherd of the flock, the minister is the undershepherd.

Christian people should know that when their pastor speaks to them of their opportunity and responsibility of inviting and welcoming into the fellowship of the church and at the Communion table all people for whom Christ died, he is acting as a real shepherd of the sheep, leading them on the way that Christ would have them go.

It would be naive to suppose that all the pastor has to do to educate his people for an all-out program of communicant integration is to make his own personal, uncompromising attitude known. Nevertheless, this is one of the first basic steps to be taken. It is a big part of the educational process and one that must season the whole program.

ENCOURAGEMENT FROM THE PEW

No matter how saintly the preacher may be, like Moses he will need his Aaron and Hur (see Ex. 17:12). Christian people must have and exercise a loving concern for their minister. If he has accepted and is living by the directive of St. Paul, "Do your best to present yourself to God as one approved, a workman who has no need to be ashamed, *rightly handling the Word of truth*" (2 Tim. 2:15), if he is fearlessly applying the law of God and the Gospel of Jesus Christ in a relevant manner to the lives of his parishioners, it is both the privilege and the responsibility of the members of his congregation to encourage and help strengthen him in his resolve.

Pastors are human beings with all their human foibles and weaknesses. They who "preach the Word" and should be "urgent in season and out of season" (2 Tim. 4:2) are not angels and sometimes lack the fortitude needed to say and do what the exigencies of the hour may require. The fear of unfavorable reaction from their superiors, their people, and the community in which they must work may keep them from speaking and acting as God's prophets. It is especially then that the priesthood of believers must be exercised by those who have been called out of darkness into God's marvelous light (1 Peter 2:9). When the pastor of the congregation is inclined to "pussyfoot" when he should be walking boldly and firmly, knowledgeable members of the flock must call upon him to be what his title implies—shepherd, leader—even when such leading will take him and them "through the valley of the shadow of death" (Ps. 23:4). Church members owe such expressed concern to all who may be involved.

THE PASTOR IDENTIFYING WITH PEOPLE

Some authorities claim that we learn more through what we see than through what we hear. Church members hear their pastor, and they see him. The message on Sunday morning is heard, but the pastor delivering the sermon is seen; and faithful church members normally want to see the pastor when he preaches. If he tells them it is within their Christian calling to identify themselves in love with people who need the fellowship of the church and with people against whom a cruel, unloving society discriminates, that is one step in a necessary educational process. But if church people *see* their pastor doing what he tells them they are to do, that too is a potent part of the educational process. Saying and doing must always go hand in hand.

In order that the pastor's words may become effective in the lives of his parishioners, they must see him identifying with members of racial or ethnic groups different from the people of the congregation or parish. This the pastor may find difficult to do.

He can knock at the doors of the church's new neighbors to invite their children to Sunday school and the adults to the church services. This approach is not to be negated. But there may be a more effective way for the pastor of the church to identify with people of a different racial or ethnic background—a way that is in keeping with an ideology on a higher plane than one which may be construed as wanting to build or save his congregation. He can seek the company of people who need fellowship and social concern because *they* need it. He can do it for their sake simply because they are human beings with whom he can identify in their known needs.

There are many avenues of approach to people for favorable contacts, which can develop into real personal friendships—a not unlikely result and one to be greatly desired.

The pastor can invite newly found acquaintances and friends to the parsonage. Later he may find it advantageous, and acceptable to those whose acquaintance and friendship are being developed, also to invite members of the congregation who would appreciate the opportunity to share with the pastor and his family the helpful experience of being in the wholesome company of people of another racial or ethnic group. Such social contacts must be sincere: they must be made because the person extending the invitation accepts those invited as persons whose acquaintance or friendship is appreciated. Although church membership can be a result, such friendship must not be cultivated merely for the sake of gaining members for the church.

ASKING THE CONGREGATION

When minority group members want to become a part of the fellowship, it is wrong to ask a congregation of fallible, sinful people—even such as have been sanctified by the Spirit of God and now constitute the church's membership—to decide this matter which has been decided in the eternal counsel of God and revealed in His Word, the Holy Scriptures. A congregation has no right to reject a person from the fellowship of Christ in the church because of his race or ethnic background. To do so is a form of idolatry—giving to men the power that belongs to God alone. To ask a congregation to vote on the eligibility of a person because of his race is equally sinful.

THE COMMON CUP

Perhaps few who accept the Lord's Supper as a communion of fellow members of the body of Christ and between Christ and the communicant will deny the fellowship aspect of the Communion when members of different racial groups, communing together, drink from the same chalice. Nevertheless, more than one congregation moving toward communicant integration has suddenly discontinued the traditional use of the common cup. No matter what type of argument may under other circumstances be used for abandoning the traditional chalice, its abandonment in anticipation of racial communicant integration not only expresses a common stereotype view—Negroes are either diseased or prone to disease—it also negates the fellowship, unity, and acceptance that the Communion itself expresses. Such a change must be opposed with all firmness. Though the changeover from the common cup to the individual cup can be sanctioned with a good theological conscience, it nevertheless denies the very nature of the church if it is done to keep nonwhite communicants from drinking out of the same cup with their white brothers and sisters.

ESTABLISHING AN INCLUSIVE COMMUNITY

A new world is fast emerging, and the church is a part of it. In horse-and-buggy days perhaps the church had a fairly adequate program for meeting the needs of an agrarian society; but those days are gone forever. Fast disappearing are the geographic communities of people living within circumscribed areas where they know one another and one another's needs and where the church as an integral part of the community can function as God's people serving men in their total human need.

A church in a neighborhood where all the members are on a plane of affluence must structure a program which moves its people in a realistic way to meet the needs of their less fortunate neighbors a little farther away. The program must be so conceived and implemented that the members will know and carry out the radical demands of truly Christian social concern for those who are less fortunate. A community, not necessarily geographic, reaching across racial and economic lines and including all people in a ministry of concern, must be reestablished.

To detail the many ways in which the individual congregational program can be structured so that the members will become identified with people of other racial backgrounds and economic conditions is impossible here. Time and local circumstances must determine the specifics. No matter what details go into the program, however, it must be grounded in and developed out of certain basic concepts of the Good News in Jesus Christ. When God in Christ became incarnate, He went all the way in identifying Himself with all men in their total need. In the fullest sense He could call them brothers and bring them reconciliation and life in its completeness, which includes the restoration of justice and equity. When God in Christ becomes incarnate in the believing Christian—"Christ in you" (Col. 1:27)—His purpose is not altered. He wants to identify Himself with all men through the one in whom He has taken up His abode. That is the type of community that the church, now largely divorced from a geographical area, must develop. That should be the blueprint of its program in this modern age of racial conflict and of poverty in the midst of plenty.

"The prayer of a righteous man has great power in its effects" (James 5:16), but the prayer of an unrighteous man will fall with a thud, unanswered, to the ground. Praying for the mission of the church in faraway places can be effective when the man who prays proves himself to be a "righteous man" in his relationship to those near at hand. A righteous man, "right" in his relationship with God and truly reconciled to God through the suffering, death, and resurrection of Jesus Christ, will pray and give and work for the mission of the church carried on in faraway places. He will demonstrate that he is indeed righteous through Jesus Christ as he identifies with the neighbor in need of his love and concern in the blighted area of the inner city and in the Negro ghetto of the metropolis where he works but from whose problems he and his family have escaped by moving to greener pastures in the outlying area of the city or in one of its suburbs.

The church in a more-favored geographic community outside the crowded inner city can become directly involved in the life of a church that is swimming in the sea of modern inner-city problems. The church that is better favored can help the less-favored one in many ways. It can help supply greatly needed financial assistance, for the average inner-city church has lost its affluent members, who are now supporting churches in more prosperous neighborhoods;

those to whom the inner-city church is ministering are the financially less fortunate ones, many of whom are not able to support the church but must be supported by it. A "drink of cold water" in the form of financial assistance will help.

Such financial assistance given by a congregation, by its auxiliaries, by individual members, or by all of them has definite limitations for both the giver and the recipient. It may act as a sop to the conscience of the giver and as an excuse to remain aloof from people who need his personal fellowship more than his dollars. Financial gifts without the donor's personal involvement may help to quiet or relieve a symptom here and there, while the disease continues to spread and the loneliness of those involved, like a threatening storm cloud, becomes more and more ominous.

THEY NEED EACH OTHER

Personal involvement wherever that is humanly possible is the great need of the church in the inner city, where the problems of slum and ghetto—crime, juvenile delinquency, dope addiction, illiteracy, and poverty—are obvious on all sides. What is more, the person living outside the inner city needs to be involved himself in the problems of the inner-city church. Inner-city people are his brothers: all of them in Adam and some of them in Christ. They need him, and he needs them. Without them he suffers, perhaps without knowing it, something of the separation between brother and brother symbolized in the story of Cain and Abel.

The affluent, middle-class brother must become conscious of his need for the needy and for personal involvement in the life and problems of the church which needs his help. If he goes to those in need in any other spirit than that of a brother who accepts his brother because he is a brother, the needy brother will sense his condescension or paternalism, and little good will be accomplished. For it is only when they meet as equals that they can be mutually helpful. When such equality is recognized and accepted, the brother from the outside can come to the church of the inner city as a brother, identify with its people, and cooperate in doing what God wants them to do together.

The Christian brother who lives in an affluent community and is a member of a church of middle-class affluent members must at this point lay aside all false humility, so that he might recognize in the gifts of God which he has in abundance the opportunity to aid his needy brothers.

PUTTING POTENTIAL TO WORK

An example. A congregation in a small Midwestern college town has among its members more than 200 university graduates, many of them men and women of experience in the church. They know its teachings and its history, its polity and administrative procedure. Many of them are themselves teachers. Although perhaps few congregations have that degree of manpower potential, nevertheless much of it is found in middle-class, well-to-do churches in suburbs and elsewhere. To the detriment of all, much of this potential remains untapped and unused in the church and its program.

These gifts of God to the church—dedication, education in many fields, and knowledge and experience in church administration—should be channeled into places where they can be used effectively. Nowhere are they needed more than in the churches in underprivileged areas of our large cities. There where it is needed most this manpower potential is lacking. Persons with dedication and know-how, who identify with the needy and the underprivileged church in the big city can be an unbounded blessing and a cause for daily thanksgiving to God on the part of the pastor and the members of the inner-city church thus blessed.

Such sharing of manpower should be a part of the program of the congregation outside the inner city. Giving, they will receive; sharing will be a source of spiritual renewal.

The miles that separate the suburbs from the inner city are no major impediment, for the expressways leading to the heart of the big city are well known and used by the suburbanite. As a link between his home and the shop, office, theater, and downtown shopping district, the expressways can also be the link with the inner-city church and the people whom the church wants to serve there.

Occasionally, families with a keenly developed social conscience have purposely moved back into the city, where they can directly identify with people of the community and their problems as well as with the church serving the community. If this were done on a larger scale, many problems that confront our big cities and their churches would diminish or be solved. The decision to make such a move must be made by the families themselves. Many circumstances will be taken into consideration; to do or not to do must be left to personal decision guided by an intelligent, enlightened social conscience that takes into consideration responsibility toward society as well as family.

ESCAPE FROM BOREDOM

Whether one likes bridge or not, who can blame a housewife who, to avoid boredom, spends hours each week playing bridge with other housewives who likewise want to escape the boredom of having nothing to do? With the many gadgets at their disposal—vacuum sweeper, dishwasher, and dryer, and a mechanical laundry installed in the home—and with meals cooked in advance by commercial concerns, who would not be bored with nothing to do? Even across-the-fence neighborhood gossip isn't sufficient pastime to relieve the weariness of having nothing meaningful to do. But whether one resorts to bridge or gossip to while away many hours of tedium, a wholesome involvement in the lives and problems of less fortunate people can be a very worthy substitute. Such involvement in social concern and activity can remove the monotony of a somewhat meaningless existence. It can substitute for housewifely boredom a feeling of exhilaration that can come only to those who have found a reason for existence outside themselves and their selfish, self-centered ego.

Adult male members of middle-class families may join a service club for several reasons, not the least of which may be to get away from the tedium of day-by-day chasing after dollars or success. Hours will be devoted to the planning of a benefit "pancake day"; and the profits will be given to some worthy and needy social welfare agency. Those more conscious of middle-age spread and the need for exercise may faithfully adhere to a schedule of so-and-so-many hours weekly on the golf course. But if the elimination of boredom is the chief objective for indulging in the sport, devoting at least some time each week to the well-being of needy people in the inner city, who have no opportunity to see a golf course (much less to take part in the sport itself), will pay dividends in several directions. What a vast vista of opportunity for social concern and service is unfolded before the gaze of middle-class, affluent people of our suburbs if they have eyes to see. What a challenge to them as citizens and, if they are Christians, as members of the kingdom of God!

Myriad are the programs that dedicated workers, professional and nonprofessional, have developed to involve their inner-city congregations in the total human needs of their communities. These programs are so varied that even a minimal description of them would go far beyond the limitations of this book. Willing Christians living outside the inner city can phone the inner-city church for information on local parish programs in which they can take part for more effective witness to Christ in the inner city. Better yet—let them visit the inner-city church and see its programs in action.

If at all possible, staff workers should live in the area of the church. Residence there can be an important symbol of a wholesome staff consecration to the members of the church and to others in the community whom the church wants to serve. But Christians living in better residential areas—who because of their membership in the body of Christ share in the responsibility of the inner-city church and give of their time and substance to the church's program development—can be instruments of the Spirit of God for reviving and strengthening the faith, hope, and spirit of these inner-city workers.

The Church as Institution

The church normally operates within the framework of an institution, a local congregation, a group of congregations of a given district, or the union of such districts in one national or international body. The institution as an organization and framework within which the church itself functions, witnessing to Christ its Head, must be distinguished from the church itself. The institution is not the end; it is a means toward an end. The end is God's ultimate purpose in creation—His own glory. The final purpose, then, for the existence of the church is the glory of God. When the church as an institution serves that end, it is good and praiseworthy. When it serves another end—mere self-perpetuation or trying to bring about conversions by power foreign to the Spirit of God—it serves a bad purpose. As the church—the body of Christ—functions in society, the purpose of the church as church and the purpose of the church as institution or organization must always be identical. The church as institution must not be downgraded; it is the instrument of the church as the body of Christ. But the church as institution must be criticized and judged whenever, like a malignant growth of wild cancer cells, it does not serve the church as the body of Christ nor the final purpose of the church's existence, the glory of God.

10

Signs of Hope on the Horizon

See, I have given you a door flung wide open.
Rev. 3:8 (Phillips)

In the 1930s, when the race question began to emerge as a major issue confronting the nation and the church, the church (as we have seen in a previous chapter) was not ready to meet the issue in true witness to Christ. Especially on the local level it is still found dragging its feet, seemingly incapable of confronting the world with the good news in Jesus Christ through word and deed in this time of unparalleled challenge. There nevertheless were and still are signs of hope on the horizon for the church.

Church Pronouncements

A historic event took place in July 1937, when a conference convened in Oxford, England, which became known as the Oxford Conference on Church, Society [or Community; see note 1], and State. Almost all the major church bodies of the world (the Roman Catholic Church excepted) were represented. Delegates from 40 countries, including the younger churches in Japan, China, India, Africa, and South America, were in attendance. Because of the Nazi regime in Germany, no representatives from the German state church were permitted to attend; some of the German Free Churches were represented by delegates who praised the new German government.

"The essential theme of the Oxford Conference . . . was the life-and-death struggle between Christian faith and the secular and pagan tendencies of our time." [1] Another conference was convened in Edinburgh, Scotland, immediately after the close of the Oxford Conference. It was known as the Edinburgh Conference on Faith and Order and was made up largely of delegates who had attended the Oxford Conference. Growing out of these two conferences, the World Council of Churches came into existence in 1948.[2]

With the presence, participation, and evident influence at the Oxford Conference of black, brown, and yellow churchmen from the far points of the compass, a good and forthright race relations pronouncement was adopted. If nothing else, it was to stimulate at least on the higher levels of the church in the United States—among officials within the Federal Council of the Churches of Christ and at national church conventions where the Oxford Conference was to be discussed—a consideration of the church's responsibility in race relations.

From the official report of the conference the following sentences, which summarize the conference's statement on "Church and Race," have been gleaned:

> For Christians, the starting point in this as in every problem of the relations of man is the affirmation that all men are by birthright children of God created in His image, and therefore brothers and sisters to one another. They are, moreover, "brothers for whom Christ died," and are intended by God to be brought within the fellowship of His one true church.
>
> There are certain principles which Christians everywhere should seek to have incorporated in the sentiments and public policies of their nations and communities. Among these are:
>
> (1) The recognition of the value of every human being as a person.
>
> (2) The right of every person, whatever his race, color or present status, to the conditions essential for life as a person; to education; to opportunity in his vocation, recreation and social intercourse.
>
> (3) Full participation in fellowship and leadership for members of a less-advanced people as they prove their ability.
>
> (4) Active cooperation and fellowship among leaders of different racial groups.
>
> (5) Recognition by the community of its responsibility to less privileged persons of whatever race or group, not only for their assistance and protection but also for special educational and cultural opportunities.
>
> (6) The necessity of such economic and social change as shall open the way to full opportunity for persons of all races.
>
> However, it is as members of the church of Christ that Christians bear the heaviest guilt for the present situation. And here is their greatest obligation and opportunity. . . .[3]

Although national conventions of some major church bodies had already taken cognizance of the ethical involvement of the Christian church in the fast-emerging race issue and had expressed their awareness of the issue, it was after the Oxford Conference that race relations pronouncements by them and others became increasingly frequent.[4]

The real breakthrough in the form of vigorous pronouncements that cover every area of the church's rightful concern, beginning with congregational integration and fanning out to all areas of responsibility in all phases of social life, came in 1946. At a meeting of the Federal Council of Churches of Christ in America held in Columbus, Ohio, in March of that year, the Committee on Church and Race presented a report which was adopted unanimously. The report, in form a pronouncement, offered to all its constituent members for consideration and possible adoption, included the following statements:

> The Federal Council of the Churches of Christ in America hereby renounces the pattern of segregation in race relations as unnecessary and undesirable and a violation of the Gospel of love and human brotherhood. Having taken this action, the Federal Council requests its constituent communions to do likewise. As proof of their sincerity in this renunciation *they will work for a non-segregated Church and a non-segregated society.*
>
> The church when true to its higher destiny, has always understood that its gospel of good news has a two-fold function, namely:
>
> To create new men with new motives.
>
> To create a new society wherein such men will find a friendly environment within which to live their Christian convictions.[5]

By 1956 all churches belonging to the council had adopted either the pronouncement or one of their own of similar import. Other national and international church bodies also adopted race relations resolutions during the same decade. It was during these years, 1946 to 1956, that many of the pronouncements of the churches gave expression for the first time to the theological concern for the total man, man as a creature of God living in society and man as a member or potential member of the society called the church.

One might assume that pronouncements are merely the expression of what Christians believe and are trying to live by even before the pronouncements have been made. But in the past in the area of race relations the church has not always witnessed to its people in keeping with its duty toward Christ; and the acceptance of pronouncements at a convention of a church body or at a bishop's conference or elsewhere is no assurance that they will be implemented on the local parish level.

Voices in the Wilderness

When John the Baptist cried out "in the wilderness of Judea," "Repent, for the kingdom of heaven is at hand" (Matt. 3:1-2), he was a minority in the church of his time. There have been minorities with a similar message ever since. Although they might not have been conscious of this their high calling in Christ, for some time there have been small minorities within the church who, like a voice in the wilderness of American white supremacy, have been calling the church to repentance and to a recognition of the nearness of the kingdom of God. They were not satisfied with pronouncements made in the high clouds of ecclesiastical and denominational officialdom; the words were good but too remote from people on earth and in the church. Pronouncements had to be brought down to earth to become flesh and bone of the body, the church. Small groups of committed people were organized within their own denominations to glorify God by stripping the barnacles of racism from the ship of the church. Though their voices were heard high up in the chambers of the mighty in the church, their feet were on the ground as they tried to change the church where it is the church: in the hearts of men and among people of the local community.

A soft-spoken, saintly man, Father John LaFarge, S. J., became the chief founder of the Catholic Interracial Council (CIC) of New York. Founded on Pentecost 1934, the council established a Catholic Interracial Center in New York City. It became "a center of information, public discussion, and assistance" to other councils similarly organized.[6] In 1959, when the CIC of New York celebrated the 25th anniversary of its founding, its *Interracial Review* reported that 36 more councils had been founded in all parts of the country, many of them south of the Mason-Dixon line.

Perhaps as an outgrowth of the CIC anniversary celebration and the compelling need of the times, a new Roman Catholic organization came into being one year later—the National Catholic Conference for Interracial Justice (NCCIJ). The conference, working out of its national office in Chicago, has as its basic task "*to service and help strengthen a locally based movement aimed at securing justice and love in human relations."*

The Lutheran Human Relations Association of America (LHRAA) was born on the campus of Valparaiso University, Valparaiso, Ind., in 1953. The association, as well as its annual institute, draws its strength and support from concerned people of the church in all sections of the country. Clergy and lay people are involved. LHRAA establishes chapters wherever a group of people of the church are interested. The association meets the challenge of race on two fronts; in the church it promotes a fellowship free of racial or ethnic barriers, and in society in general it helps eliminate racial or ethnic discrimination. The association has helped bring about meaningful pronouncements by its own denomination and has tried with some success to move the national body to greater involvement in the race issue. LHRAA, like NCCIJ, is committed to *the primary task of reaching and helping the church on the local level to identify itself more fully with the cause of racial and ethnic justice.*

The Episcopal Society for Cultural and Racial Unity (ESCRU) was organized in December 1959 at Raleigh, N. C., primarily under the leadership of the Rev. John B. Morris, who became the executive director. The society's purpose is "to encourage men to respond positively to God's call for unity in the church. The unity of God with man and man with man is made by God in Baptism and Holy Communion. We commit ourselves to establish total participation in the church for all persons without regard to race, class, or national origin; to give mutual support to all who act in this ministry of reconciliation; and *to express this concern at parish levels and in a more creative community at large.*"[7] ESCRU, too, organizes local chapters "to express this concern at parish levels."

Two associations of similar purpose were organized in other denominations: the Presbyterian Interracial Council in 1963 and the Baptist Association for Racial Brotherhood in 1964.

The organizations mentioned above have dared to speak the unpopular word and to do the unwanted deed that would call for the elimination of racism from and by the church.

Quakers and Jews

The social concern and the resulting humanitarian activity of Quakers generally, as well as the absence of racial discrimination among their own rank and file, are attested in the pages of American history. Their humanitarian concern, while motivated by a more ambiguous and less defined theology, is evident wherever Quakers function and is in sharp contrast to the lack of expression of a similar concern among members of major denominational groups that have a more highly developed and articulated theology.

When the historic National Conference on Religion and Race convened in Chicago in January 1963, a total of 18 of the 67 organizations represented were Jewish. Deep Jewish concern and commitment prompted a percentage of participation far greater than that of other church or church-related organizations. Two of these Jewish organizations, the Anti-Defamation League of B'nai B'rith and the American Jewish Committee, are particularly well known for their direct and continued involvement in race relations. Literature of high caliber and scientific accuracy flows ceaselessly from the offices of these organizations and is available to Christians and Jews alike, much of it free of charge.

Beyond Words to the Deed

Under the courageous leadership of Father John Morris of ESCRU, an integrated group of 28 priests set out by bus from New Orleans in September 1962 on a dramatic prayer pilgrimage to the Protestant Episcopal Church convention in Detroit. When they arrived at the Jackson, Miss., bus terminal and tried to use its facilities together, they were arrested and thrown into jail.

The Lutheran Women's Missionary League, an auxiliary of The Lutheran Church – Missouri Synod, had scheduled its 1955 convention for New Orleans, where segregated facilities were to be used. As a result of the stand taken by the Lutheran Human Relations Association of America, the convention was canceled. Although the cancellation of the convention caused some bitterness and much disappointment at first, it was soon hailed as a mark of progress, and conventions since then have been held on an integrated basis.

Dr. Martin Luther King, Jr., was invited to come to Albany, Ga., to help its Negro citizens beleaguered by the destructive forces of segregation. After meeting with the leaders of what was called the Albany Movement, and with their cooperation, Dr. King invited religious leaders from other parts of the nation to come to the assistance of the oppressed Negroes of Albany. Ninety persons came from the New York City and Chicago areas to identify themselves with the Albany Negroes in their struggle. As they assembled in dignity, peacefully and orderly, in front of the city hall, they were arrested. Some of them spent as many as six days in jail, until $200 bail money was paid for each of them.

The civil rights march on Washington, D. C. (Aug. 28, 1963), took place one year to the day after the incarceration of the religious leaders in Albany. Among the 200,000 marchers were thousands of clergymen as well as lay representatives of churches and other religious organizations.

While the historic 87-day civil-rights filibuster was in progress in 1964, some 6,000 clergymen from many parts of the nation came to the capitol in Washington, D. C., in a great religious rally emphasizing their moral concern for enactment of an effective civil rights law.

A civil rights demonstration that shocked the nation into greater awareness of the seriousness of our segregation practices and, as President Johnson said, helped to arouse the national conscience was the Selma-to-Montgomery march in March 1965. Many clergy and other professional church workers, besides thousands of other Christian-motivated persons, were among the 20,000 who took part in the march through racially dangerous Dallas County.

In addition to the more corporate actions described above, during this period of revolutionary change many individuals within the church, especially many clergymen, translated good words into good deeds by identifying with the oppressed and taking the cross of suffering upon themselves.

One example is that of the Rev. Joseph W. Ellwanger of Birmingham, Ala. On March 6, 1965, the day before the brutal actions of Alabama state troopers focused the nation's attention on Selma, and when the march to Montgomery was scheduled to begin, this young Lutheran clergyman led some 70 concerned white citizens of Alabama, amid the jeers and abusive language of segregationist onlookers, to the Dallas County courthouse in Selma. There he read a statement of concern: "We as white citizens of Alabama have come to Selma today to tell the nation that there are white people in Alabama who will speak out against the events which have recently occurred in this and neighboring counties and towns."

The pastor of a downtown Baptist church in a Southern community recommended to his congregation that they receive Negroes into membership. When they refused, he and 10 members of the congregation transferred their membership to a church which had formerly been all Negro.

As early as 1941 the pastor of a Baptist church in Albany, Ga., tried to help relieve tensions there by bringing city officials and local Negro leaders together. When racial tension mounted in the summer of 1962, militant segregationists within his congregation tried to secure his signature to a petition calling for writing segregation into the church's constitution. He refused and vigorously opposed circulation of the petition.

In 1956, when Clinton, Tenn., was in an uproar over a court injunction calling for integration of its schools, the pastor of the largest Baptist church, amid many threats, led nine Negro children to the school that was to be integrated.

In 1957, in spite of an angry mob, four white ministers accompanied the first Negro students to be enrolled in Little Rock's Central High School.

In November 1960 the Rev. Lloyd Foreman, accompanied by a Roman Catholic priest, escorted his 5-year-old daughter through a vicious crowd to William Frantz Elementary School, the first public school to be integrated in New Orleans. He also helped hesitant white mothers in and out of the school building until the boycott of the school began to crumble.

When nine Negroes were turned away from worship services at a Methodist church in Jackson, Miss., the pastor and assistant pastor in protest sought and were granted transfers to other parishes.

William Stringfellow, a Harvard Law School graduate, chose upon graduation to move to Harlem to work there as a lawyer, to take some part in the politics of the community, and to become a member of the church there. He reportedly renders his professional services to worthy persons, representing them in court regardless of their inability to pay for his services. In what he says and does he witnesses to Christ in a martyrlike way and thus represents the church well, though it is his contention that he is "only a Christian layman using his vocation as a lawyer to help and to discipline human beings who are downtrodden."

Clergymen in an Urban Society

The time was when the minister of the church was an integral part of the community. Society was largely agrarian. The life of the community centered in the church. The parish priest or minister was an identified part of the community and its day-by-day living. He was known by all, and if he responded to community needs in keeping with what was expected of him, he was always accessible. In such a simple society, devoid of the complexities of urban industrialization, it was not too difficult for him to identify himself with the people and to minister to the total man—to temporal as well as spiritual needs. Symbolic of this community relationship of pastor and people was the seedtime ritual. During the 3 days following the Fifth Sunday After Easter (in the church calendar called Rogation [prayer] Sunday), "the faithful would proceed from the churches into the fields, chanting litanies. Prayers would be offered for the growth of the fruits of the field and for the tiller of the ground, asking God's blessing on the plants that rose with the spring awakening." [8] The priest or the pastor, with the mind of Christ, could extend his new life as a baptized believer to others through the *kerygma* (the good words of the goodness of Christ) which he spoke and through the *agape* (love) life that he lived. As an imitator of Christ (Eph. 5:1-2) he set an example for the flock to follow.

A crying need of the church in this century is to gain some type of community living in a complex, urban, industrialized society, where the tragic loss of community is symbolized in the conflicts between street gangs of the inner cities of the United States. "In the rapid transformation of the United States from a rural people to an industrial society, a change which has been completed during the lifetime of the older communicants of our parishes, the rise of the Giant City (megalopolis) has come to be of marked importance." It now presents a "scene of unplanned obsolescence" in which many of our institutions, developed to meet the needs of a society that was predominantly rural, are of very limited service today. The churches in their present institutional structure "seldom serve as 'the conscience of society.' Rather, themselves committed to and bound by institutional patterns developed in a rural setting, they often find themselves suffering the indignity of painful and guilty irrelevance." [9] This irrelevance is most obvious in the church's inability to deal responsibly with the race issue.

Hope for the church is evidenced, nevertheless, in the theological understanding, concern, and commitment of many younger ministers in various denominations. They have witnessed the futility and hypocrisy of racism as it ruled or was condoned in the church. Racism, discrimination, and segregation are contrary to their deepest theological insights. For them these aberrations within the institutional church are not "purely social matters," as they were for many in earlier decades, but rather a truly theological problem involving cardinal doctrines of the Christian faith. If these young ministers were to condone segregation or any of its corollaries, they would be disavowing much to which they were committed by their ordination vow. There is hope indeed for the church in these younger, theologically motivated clergy.

The Ecumenical and Liturgical Movements

The times point to two needs: a real togetherness or acceptance on the part of lonely human beings, and a power beyond themselves and their science to bring them together. The church claims to have both—a God who can unite brother with brother, and the unity itself. The church has been saying this all along: God in Christ unites brother with brother to the glory of God.

Of all the things that hinder the church in its witness to Christ, especially in the non-Western world, there is perhaps no obstacle greater than the many divisions within the church. There is disunity between the East and the West, between nation and nation; there is a cleavage between whites and nonwhites on a global basis; in the United States racial conflict is raging. It is the church's responsibility to help resolve this conflict between brother and brother in our land and bring to a disunited world, in many places carrying on fratricidal warfare, the fellowship of acceptance which it confesses and preaches. In the church's disunited state, though, its deeds of disunity speak so loudly that its words cannot get through. The witness to Christ must be made on all possible levels of social life. To disclaim responsibility for or to disregard the witness to Christ on one level negates the witness on other levels and makes a meaningful contribution to wholesome community living impossible.

"You shall be called the repairer of the breach" (Is. 58:12) is not merely a nice-sounding statement that God makes about those who have been called by His name. It describes them in their new vocation. It is at the same time a directive to do the deed. The repairer of the breach cannot choose which of the breaches he would repair. Rather, all brokenness is to be restored to wholeness. Man on every level of existence is to be united with his fellowman in a brotherhood intended by God in the creation. The ecumenically minded folk in the church's midst who, to the glory of God and the restoration of creation, would repair the breach wherever it may be found, who would use the cement of the new life in Christ and the tool of the Spirit of God to repair the breach, are an evidence that God has not abandoned His people. These breach repairers are a ray of hope coming through the dark clouds of troublous times. There are many of them. They are found within all the major church denominations; also the pope at Rome has been influenced by them. Their voices are heard, and they are found wherever, in the church and in the world surrounding it, efforts toward peace and unity are being made.

A blessing that is coming out of the modern world confusion, then, is an awakening on the part of many within the church to their high calling in Christ to be "repairers of the breach" that separates man from man in any human situation.

A second blessing resulting from this human dilemma is a recognition on the part of men of their helplessness in their own strength to reunite man with man and of their need for strength and power from outside themselves to effect those changes in man's relationship to man in the church and in the world, which the exigencies of our times call for and the unity of heaven and earth require. That power outside man is God the Creator Himself.

It is the intent of the founders of the modern liturgical movement to renew emphasis on the worship of the church "as expressive of the implications of Christian action in personal and social life." [10] The liturgical movement, according to a Roman Catholic authority, "has as its aim the cultivation of corporate, communal worship by means of the historic forms of liturgy which are a part of our common Christian tradition. By so interpreting these liturgies in their original meaning and purpose as expressions of the deepest bonds uniting us as Christians to God and to one another, the movement seeks a focal center in the liturgy for our religious inspiration and common activity, *not only in the Church, but also in our life in the world.*

It seeks to bring back in the Church's life certain ideals and practices of worship in her inherited treasures of the past which have been obscured, forgotten, or dormant; and in turn, to apply these ideals and practices in a constructive way to the issues of a modern Christian society." [11] The same authority claims the reason for the appeal of this revived interest in worship and liturgy "is not due solely to historical scholarship and the love of beautiful forms and symbols" but to "the essential purpose of liturgy itself, when properly understood, namely, the integration of all of life under the Lordship of Christ." [12] "Advocates of liturgical renewal want to take the total man, body and soul, and unite him with his brothers in Christ, worshipping the Father through the Son in the Holy Spirit." [13]

The ecumenical and the liturgical movements point to the brokenness of human society when some kind of social cohesion is a *sine qua non,* and they then point the Christian to the unity in Christ and to Christ as the source of God's power to effect unity.

The Negro Church

For generations there have been congregations of Negro membership in organic union and in fellowship with the major denominations. The term "Negro church" as here used has reference to those Negro churches that are organized independent of the major denominations.

The Negro church is an institution developed to serve Negroes in a pluralistic society. If the term "church" as it is used in the New Testament is understood, the Negro church is self-contradictory. A church, according to the New Testament, is a fellowship or a togetherness of believers in Jesus Christ, and since there are and should be people of every racial and ethnic background in the church, an institution intended to serve but one racial group is a violation of what God intends to accomplish in the world through the redemption wrought by Jesus Christ.

In our historical development white society made it very clear that Negroes were not to enter into and be absorbed by the culture that was emerging on our soil, and Negroes were not to be assimilated into the life and fellowship of the church as an institution. The church in the United States has always been a free institution in the sense that people can choose to be or not to be members of it. Many Negroes chose to be members. But when they were rebuffed again and again and the very essence of membership—fellowship—was denied them, they withdrew and formed a protest movement, which is the Negro church. Perhaps there was no alternative for them.

On another level of existence there was no opportunity for Negroes to choose not to belong. By virtue of their being born in the United States, they were identified with the United States. When the white citizenry turned them away from that way of life which was their natural inheritance, the Negro church became the institution out of which a way of life developed for them.

> As the result of the elimination of Negroes from the political life of the American community, the Negro church became the arena of their political activities. The church was the main area of social life in which Negroes could aspire to become leaders of men.
>
> . . . Since the Negro was an outsider in the American community, it was the church that enlisted his deepest loyalties. . . . For the Negro masses, in their social and moral isolation in American society, the Negro church community has been a nation within a nation.[14]

Until several decades ago the theology of the Negro church, at least in its outward structure, was "other worldly." Prominent in the sermons were the concepts of sin, divine retribution, repentance, eternal salvation, sinful man and a righteous and holy God, and how man can be restored to God's favor and acceptance. There has now been a definite shift in emphasis to a theology that stresses the here and now. There has been a secularization of outlook because of the urbanization of Negroes, and the church has reflected this change. The established Negro churches now place increasing emphasis on the economic, social, and political problems of Negroes in this world.

If judged by the literature and other public expressions of the Negro clergy in recent years, the logical conclusion is that their theology is weak in certain fundamental areas, especially Christology. Mitigating circumstances have contributed to this weakness. A major circumstance partly responsible is the inadequate training of the Negro clergy. The chief fault of that training is not a lack of academic excellence in the schools attended by Negroes, though there was much of that, but rather the isolation in that training from the mainstream of the church's tradition and life.

Another possible reason for the lack of an adequate Christology was the contrast, not always completely understood by the Negroes themselves, between their own lives of abject poverty in a land of overflowing plenty and the obvious abundance of their white fellow Christians. It is small wonder that in such a socioreligious environment the social implications of the Gospel of Jesus Christ became a predominant emphasis. While the lack of a well-articulated Christology is to be deplored and must be corrected before the cause of the church of Jesus Christ can be adequately served, the rediscovery on the part of Negro churchmen of the importance of the social implications of the Gospel can make a significant breakthrough for the church, helping to make the teachings of Christianity relevant in these days of worldwide revolutionary change.

Since 1956 the Negro church has begun to flex its muscles, and its strength for church and nation has become visible for all to see. One would have to be totally blind not to be able to see the great role Negro clergymen and Negro congregations have played in the civil rights struggle, beginning with the Montgomery bus boycott in 1955. Leadership has come from such men as Dr. Martin Luther King, Jr., Dr. Ralph Abernathy, the Rev. Fred Shuttlesworth, the Rev. Wyatt Tee Walker, the Rev. Andrew Young, and many more. In Albany, Ga., Birmingham, Ala., Jackson and McComb counties, Miss., New York, Philadelphia, Washington, D. C., and other places, Negro churches have been the gathering points and the educational centers for the civil rights action program. Because of the use of these churches in this struggle, many of them have been destroyed—a destruction symbolic of the hatred directed against those who were occupants of pulpit and pew. Whatever truth compels us to say about the theological weakness of the Negro church, we must in the interest of the same truth acknowledge the great role it has played in the struggle for the achievement of justice for all.

Social and economic security for the Negro still remains a strong sociological reason for the continued existence of the Negro church. It is improbable that Negro churchmen in general will seek to dissolve this institution until such time as color consciousness and racial restrictions in the "white" churches are eliminated. The time should come when the church will accept its full responsibility toward Negroes by accepting them in wholehearted fellowship and working with them also in the cause of human justice.

The ongoing responsibility of the church must be the removal of those external and internal elements in the life of the church that make the continuation of the Negro church necessary. Until this goal is accomplished, it is possible that, in fulfillment of the prophetic word "the last shall be first," the Negro church may lead the church as a whole toward spiritual cleansing and renewal so that it can speak to the great nonwhite world with prophetic insight and power.

The Younger Churches of the Non-Western World

The younger churches of Asia and Africa are the result of modern missionary endeavor. When the churches of Europe and the United States of America came to these people, they were often accompanied or preceded by European colonial and imperialistic authority and control. At the same time the commercial or mercenary interests of the European nations were involved. In all too many cases—understandably so—the military and the mercenary were identified with the missionary. The good news of Jesus Christ nevertheless came through in many places, so that new churches among non-European, nonwhite people came into existence.

Since World War I and increasingly since World War II the peoples of Asia and Africa have been gaining political independence. Colonialism and imperialism of the 19th-century variety have largely vanished; at least they have been withdrawn from Asian and most African territory. The Christian church in those lands is no longer protected or supported by European colonial powers; nor can it be identified with those powers. These secular and sometimes antichristian accretions to the church are no longer present. The church in these lands must now stand or fall according to the real claims of Christianity.

Few within the churches of the United States were conscious of this unhappy alliance between missionary endeavor and the foreign political power in control of the land. But the people of those countries, especially their leaders, were conscious of it. That the good news of Jesus Christ was heard at all under such circumstances is an evidence of its divine power; and that churches came into existence in those lands is nothing less than a mystery, the miraculous work of the Spirit of God.

Some of the churches which might be considered in this connection are: India Evangelical Lutheran Church, Church of South India, Andhra Evangelical Lutheran Church, United Church of Northern India and Pakistan, Huria Kristen Batak Protestant Church, Presbyterian Church of Korea, United Church of Christ in the Philippines, Église Évangelique du Cameroun, Presbyterian Church of East Africa, Manianga Matadi Evangelical Church (Congo), Bantu Congregational Church in South Africa, Nippon Kirisuto Kyodan (United Church of Christ in Japan), and Japan Evangelical Lutheran Church. They are indeed churches under the cross, living out their lives in lands of paganism where their fellow countrymen are alien to the kingdom of God; and the alienation may sometimes be nurtured and sustained by the memories of the circumstances under which the church was introduced and brought into their midst.

If the church of Jesus Christ is in this world always a church under the cross and if what St. Paul said—"When I am weak, then I am strong" (2 Cor. 12:10)—has its application here, is it possible that God's strength may be manifested in and through these weak, younger churches of Asia and Africa (2 Cor. 12:9)? On the whole they are weak according to certain traditional church standards in the U. S. A. They are in many instances weak in theological sophistication and in numerical and financial strength, and so often they are but tolerated by those who are now in governmental authority and hence are without the protection and security that the church in the United States enjoys.

Is God preparing these churches for Kingdom activity for which He has found the established churches of the West wanting? Will the Spirit-guided leadership for the church of the future come from the heretofore largely unfruitful fields of Asia and Africa? Is it possible that the renewal of the church for which many Christians have been hoping and praying will come from the younger churches? There are signs pointing in that direction.

The traumatic effect of Nazism upon many churches and churchmen influenced the prophetic statement that came out of the Oxford Conference of 1937. But another very significant influence was the presence and participation at the conference of churchmen representing the younger churches of Asia and Africa.

A similar thing happened at the 1959 convention of The Lutheran Church—Missouri Synod, when the India Evangelical Lutheran Church requested that it be accepted into fellowship with the Missouri Synod as a sister church. With a true understanding of the nature of the church and with prophetic vision, the Rev. B. H. Jackayya, then general secretary of the India Evangelical Lutheran Church, reminded The Lutheran Church—Missouri Synod that Christianity claims loyalty to the one holy Christian and apostolic church over loyalty to a specific denomination.

At the General Conference of the Methodist Church the possible future relationship between the mother church in the U. S. A. and the younger churches in traditionally non-Christian countries was presented by Bishop Gerald Kennedy:

> The time has come when regional churches, some of them still receiving considerable financial leadership support from the American and European churches, are making contributions to the older churches. Their fresh vision often makes plain what has become blurred to us, and their experiences are often a judgment upon us. According to the New Testament promise, our giving now becomes the happy privilege of receiving, and we pray that we may see how much of what God would give us is coming to us by way of the new churches in Asia, Africa and Latin America.[15]

Upon his return from a mission study trip that took him to many countries in the non-Western world, a professor of missions at Concordia Seminary in St. Louis, in a slightly different context, wrote words that have their application here:

> We do not know how God may reach into the history of our own time—perhaps even with nuclear destruction in the West—to set the churches of Asia and Africa free from Western denominational and fiscal control so that the Gospel may become truly at home in the non-Western world.
>
> This may be at one and the same time God's visitation on our lack of missionary obedience and His way of freeing His Gospel so that it may have free course in all the world, as we pray in the Collect for the Church. We build our

temples as did the Jews and, just possibly, for destruction.[16]

Luther is quoted as comparing the advance of the Gospel with a *Platzregen,* a passing or local shower. At first the church flourished in the basin of the Mediterranean. From there the church moved northward into Europe, and from there to the Western hemisphere. Where will it move next? Are there signs pointing in the direction of Asia and Africa, to the younger churches? Are these churches of Asia and Africa destined by God to become the preachers on the housetops (Matt. 10:27), the tower of strength to save the church from the destructive forces obtaining in the institution in which it now exists? Are the younger churches a ray of hope for the whole church?

Having pointed to the rays of light and hope trying to penetrate the dark clouds, one cannot in honesty overlook the reality of the clouds themselves. The church of the 20th century has a long, long way to go before it can say that it has completely shed from its eyes the scales of racial prejudice, before it can stand unashamed before the world, witnessing to Christ in vigorous pursuit of an inclusive fellowship in the church and evenhanded justice in all of society for all people.

Fire from the Throne

I came to cast fire upon the earth, and would that it were already kindled!

Luke 12:49

Racial Crisis — a Judgment of God

As long as the church of Jesus Christ is among men, God in all His saving grace is there. His mercy shall never fail. When all but hidden from sight, it comes through the dark clouds as rays of hope.

With all the forces at work militating against racial segregation, it would seem clear that the cards are stacked against legal and/or formal segregation in society in general as well as in the church. It is becoming increasingly unpopular — except in some Southern communities — to hold out for segregation in the church. The church, by virtue of its claim to spiritual values, is compelled to take spiritual inventory, not just once a year but continually. The church will have to confront itself, while moving toward a more liberal racial attitude, with the question why.

Is the progress in the church real progress, or is it an old form of conforming to the world in a new dress — this time doing the right thing for the wrong reason? That alone is progress in the church which is spiritual, not merely institutional. God's purpose as He moves in history, through acts of judgment and deeds of mercy, is man's spiritual renewal and the evidence of such renewal in lives lived to His glory. The purpose of God and the life of the church must be identical.

The race issue is both the judgment of God and a crisis. It is a crisis unparalleled in modern history. (Crisis is the Greek word for judgment.) And there is a triple time-content for the kingdom of God and the judgment of God. From the beginning God has been both King and Judge; He is that in every crisis that moves across the pages of history; and He will be both King and Judge at the final crisis, when Christ will "come again with glory to judge both the quick and the dead."

Who knowing the present worldwide race issue to be a crisis of magnitudinous proportions, who with any knowledge at all of the church's involvement in the crisis and of the nature of the judgment of God, could deny that the racial crisis is a judgment of God upon the church? But has the time not come for God to withdraw His judgment? Is there not ample evidence of repentance and a courageous effort on the part of many to improve the image of the church by a faithful witness to Christ, even a witness involving, in many instances, suffering and, for some, death?

Abraham pleaded with the Lord that if ten righteous persons were found in Sodom, that wicked city be spared from destruction. And the Lord answered Abraham, "For the sake of ten I will not destroy it" (Gen. 18:32). More than ten righteous people for some time now have been praying, in the words of the General Prayer, "Grant . . . health and prosperity to all that are in authority, especially to the President and Congress of the United States . . . and to all our Judges and Magistrates, and endue them with grace to rule after Thy good pleasure, to the maintenance of righteousness and to the hindrance and punishment of wickedness, that we may lead a quiet and peaceable life in all godliness and honesty."

With the enactment into law on July 2, 1964, of the civil rights bill (H. R. 7152), and with all three branches of the Federal Government now committed to the eradication of racism, it would seem that at least a part of the foregoing petition has been answered or is in the process of being answered. But prayers are necessary still; the time of racial peace has not as yet arrived, either at home or abroad. The crisis is still with us, and the judgment of God is still upon the church. When will judgment end and mercy begin? God alone knows. He is the Judge. Judgment begins with Him, and it is He who must, in His good time, bring it to an end.

There is purpose in every act of God. And His purpose in the world is not unrelated to His purpose for the church. The church came forth out of the womb of His mercy; and the purpose of judgment is that mercy may once again come through. If God's mercy in Christ is understood, it may well be that to save the church He will first have to destroy it. That is the blueprint of salvation for the individual, and that is the way of salvation for the church. It is always through death to life. This dying and rising again to newness of life (Rom. 6:4) is not a once-for-all event. It is the continuing cycle of the new life in Christ: judgment brings death, and mercy brings life. This side of the grave and eternity the individual Christian and the church always need both – judgment and mercy.

For a long time now, God in infinite patience has permitted men to build an institution called the church, ostensibly to His glory. But for centuries the institution has been prone to save itself. The church's racial sins in the 20th century are of a piece with the sins of the church in the days of Constantine and of Charlemagne, in the days of the Crusades and in the days of the inhuman treatment of the Jews. Sin is always the same, different in expression but one in essence. Man sins when to save himself he denies God, the source of life; and this is done by selfishly seeking his own advantage to the detriment of his fellowman. The church sins too when, in trying to save the institution, it causes and permits others to suffer rather than taking the cross upon itself, dying if need be that it might through God in Christ live a new life.

When reviewing the patience of God toward the church in the past 1,500 years, we may plead for God's continued patience and mercy and that He would remove the crises that threaten the church. But who is man to tell God, "It is now high time that You withdraw the crises and the divine judgment involved, so that the institution we have built up for Your glory and the establishment of Your kingdom may continue in peace, prosperity, and strength"?

Signs on the Eastern Horizon

As the church prays for mercy, what are the signs of the times, and how are they to be interpreted? Is God's judgment upon the church to cease or to increase? If it is to continue, what form will it take, and what will be its purpose?

The way in which the judgment of God comes is not always the same. Sometimes it comes dramatically: the 40-year wilderness journey, the Babylonian exile, the destruction of Jerusalem. Many happenings in current history point to an even more dramatic expression of the judgment of God upon the church as an institution.

The term "fire" is sometimes used in the Scriptures to symbolize the judgment of God. As fire consumes and destroys, so also divine judgment; it destroys and will destroy all that opposes His will and purpose: ". . . lest My wrath go forth like fire and burn with none to quench it" (Jer. 4:4). Other passages of similar content are: "Under His glory a burning will be kindled, like the burning of fire. The Light of Israel will become a fire, and His Holy One a flame; and it will burn and devour his thorns and briers in one day" (Is. 10:16b-17). "The Lord God was calling for a judgment by fire." (Amos 7:4)

Are the destructive forces of the judgment of God upon the organized church *fire from the throne,* visible to those who can discern the signs of the times?

The time was when many thought that those still outside the pale of Christianity, the hundreds of millions of so-called colored peoples of the earth, the people of Asia and Africa, were anxiously waiting for the church to bring them the good news of the Gospel. All that was lacking was missionaries to be sent and dollars to hurry them on their way, and as soon as the church could "beef up" its missionary program the banner of the cross would be waving in triumph over the continents where in the past it had hardly been seen. If there ever was reason for such optimism, there is none today. Throughout Africa and especially in Asia, "Christianity is regarded as the ethnic religion of the West, and at its door is laid responsibility for all that the Western powers do. Therefore it is confidently asserted by many that Christianity leads to war, aggression, and colonial exploitation. It is responsible for the misuse of science and technology and for the present threat of atomic annihilation hanging over mankind. It is responsible for the whole mess in which the world now finds itself, and it is incapable of leading mankind to a just, stable, peaceful world order. It preaches brotherhood and unity, but does not practice it. It is not only divided into innumerable sects which prey upon one another, but introduces divisiveness into the new nations which so sorely need unity." [1]

Is God the Lord of history, and is He working in these dreadful times? If He is, what is a logical interpretation of His purpose as the institutional church in Asia and Africa finds its back pressed harder and harder against the wall?

The dilemma in which the church finds itself as it honestly faces the facts about its mission outreach in the non-Western world is not lessened as it recalls its race relations history in the United States; and the statement, credited to Dr. Charles S. Johnson and spoken before the end of the first half of this century, is still true: "The most segregated hour in the week is eleven o'clock on Sunday morning." In fact, what is happening in the United States is in a large measure responsible for the status of the church still identified with the West but trying to live out its life in the non-Western world. With racial segregation still entrenched in the church in the United States and opposition to the mission program of the church in the non-Western world growing—and the two together presenting a dilemma of staggering proportions—one wonders: is God still a part of the whole? Is He working out a divine blueprint according to a divine purpose? Christian faith responds that He is and that His judgment is somehow involved in all of it.

The Hammer and the Sickle

There is some truth in the rather naive statement made by a church official: "How wicked those communists are; they are destroying the church!" But the wickedness of the communists as well as the destruction that they are bringing upon the church need some critical analysis unless one would rule God completely out of the picture of world happenings.

Whether one is justified or not in affixing the adjective "wicked" to the names and the theories of Mao Tse-tung, Nikita Khrushchev, Stalin, Lenin, and Karl Marx, it could also be said that Nebuchadnezzar, Cyrus, and the 10 elder brothers of Joseph were wicked. But in a sense all of them, perhaps unwittingly, were or are God's servants.

Nebuchadnezzar became the punitive instrument in the hands of God to take the people of Judea and Jerusalem into the Babylonian exile. In doing so, he became God's servant: "Now I have given all these lands into the hand of Nebuchadnezzar, the king of Babylon, My *servant*." (Jer. 27:6; see also Is. 44:28–45:1; Gen. 50:20.)

If prophets like Isaiah or Jeremiah were to arise today, they might give the title "servant of God" to Karl Marx, Lenin, Joseph Stalin, Nikita Khrushchev, and Mao Tse-tung; for *God may be accomplishing His purposes in the world through the communist revolution.*

The revolution had its beginning on that day in October 1917 when a shot was fired from the bow of the cruiser *Aurora* in Leningrad harbor within walking distance of the winter palace of the Czar of Russia. It began then, and though only five decades have passed since, communism has spread throughout eastern Europe and far into Asia; it has gained hegemony over countries in the Near East and northern Africa; it has established beachheads in the Western Hemisphere; and its loyal disciples are found in almost every land. Although based upon a profound philosophy, it has several popularly understood purposes: capitalism must be destroyed; the land and all the good things of the earth must become the common property of the proletariat, the working people; science must be enthroned; and religion, "the opium of the masses," must be wiped out.

The shot from the *Aurora* got it started, but the communist revolution had a number of causes that antedate it. They are centered in the social and economic conditions of the masses of the 18th and 19th centuries. For generations, under czarist, tyrannical rule, millions of the Russian people lived out their lives as serfs, in ignorance and poverty, and what they had of this world's goods was obtained through slavelike labor and was sufficient, at best, to sustain them on a bare subsistence level.

The industrial revolution, with the exploitation of the natural resources of many lands and the development of a capitalistic society, brought about a large middle class—bourgeoisie—with living standards unknown and perhaps undreamed of by their forebears, while the great bulk of profits flowed into the coffers of industrial magnates who made up a very small percentage of the population.

When serfdom held millions of people in its cruel grasp and when depersonalized and equally inhuman industrialization made of the lower classes in England, Europe, and the United States an unenviable example of man's inhumanity to man, the organized church was there all the time, either cooperating with the power structure or condoning its practices or being apathetic to the crying needs of the masses and contenting itself with working merely for personal regeneration.

It is in the context of the socioeconomic system described above that Marxism and the Bolshevik revolution came into being, and communism is now spreading rapidly over the earth. One of the reasons why communism can be called a Christian heresy is that *it is a criticism of the failure of the Christian churches to carry out an essential part of their task.* A heresy arises when the church drastically fails to fulfill its function and at the same time refuses because of obstinacy or blindness to admit its failure and to be corrected." [2]

ATHEISTIC COMMUNISM—A RELIGION

Although communism is an avowed enemy of religion, it is itself a religion. For those who understand, accept, and live for it, communism apparently fills a need common to man which organized religion was not able to supply. What Christ said when He rebuked the Tempter in the wilderness, who would have had Him make bread His all, is universally and eternally true: "Man shall not live by bread alone" (Matt. 4:4). Though the faithful Communist Party member is—devoted to dialectical materialism, he is deeply religious and in that sense "spiritual."

Man, created in the image of God to serve and to glorify Him, must have God or a god whom he can serve and glorify. This is as much a part of his being as the desire to eat and drink. Man, instinctively dependent upon God, needs to be attached to Him at all times if he is to have security and peace and a reason for being. With God ruled out of his life by atheistic, dialectical materialism, the faithful Communist Party member finds his god in the utopian classless society which shall shortly appear; it is just beyond the horizon. He must have faith in his god and hope for his imminent appearing; he must serve him with all his heart and soul and mind. In his concern for the underdog, the communist is serving his god; and his concern is a deeply religious one.

Written and verbalized Christian theology, beautiful and costly churches and cathedrals overflowing with worshipers, and the sending of missionaries to pagan lands will not disturb the communists too greatly. What they would fear most would be a God incarnate in men who through men would live and die for men in all their known temporal needs. In other words, if Christians everywhere would live and die for the alleviation of human need and suffering and for the establishment of justice, the communists no doubt could be routed. They would see God as He truly is—alive; and the god whom they in their godless state have created in the image of man would turn out to be "the opium of the people," a figment of a frustrated mind.

In a speech delivered Sept. 1, 1957, released by Father Owen McGrath of Columban Fathers Seminary in Milton, Mass., on the seventh anniversary of its delivery, the then junior senator from Massachusetts, John F. Kennedy, said: "The Communists fear Christianity more as a way of life than as a weapon. In short, there is room in a totalitarian system for churches—but there is no room for God."

Like the church official who lamented the destruction of the church by the communists, that type of Christian anticommunist who denies the sincerity of the communist concern for the underdog in society and for the elimination of racial segregation and discrimination in our land is denying a vital truth about communism and, in so doing, becomes himself a propagator of that which he so ardently tries to oppose; for to render effective opposition to the enemy, it is above all necessary to understand him.[3]

The communist faith is attractive to so many minds because there is in it

> an appeal to the poor and the downtrodden. The doctrine holds that, poor as the workers may seem, their present disability is only temporary. They are actually participants in a dialectical process which is destined to elevate them and lower their capitalistic competitors. This is not a dream, the ideology states, but a scientific fact as demonstrable as the laws of motion. . . . The poor workers are thus actors in a cosmic drama.
>
> [The communist system] involves great evils. Often it makes for a wholly ruthless spirit and political intransigence. In most instances it involves a denial of freedom, in the sense of political freedom or freedom of expression. . . . The ugly features, involved in what is called a police state, seem to be inherent in the system. But it is clear that there are millions of individuals who accept these evils gladly because the theory so dignifies their lives. They are part of something big; they are coming into their inheritance; they are fulfilling their destiny. And, accordingly, they will work long hours, fight in the bitter cold and undergo all hardships. Their creed is manifestly an inadequate one, but we should be stupid indeed were we to allow this fact to blind us to the remarkable lift which the creed introduces into common life. We have the freedom of expression, but we do not have the *lift.*[4]

The lift nevertheless is available, the lift that men need to live responsibly, with true hope and purpose. It is to be found in the church. Because Christ is there, the *lift* is there. It may seem at first glance that to quote the following words of Christ at this place is at best inappropriate: "I, when I am *lifted* up from the earth, will draw all men to Myself" (John 12:32). He had reference to His being lifted up on the cross. But in His death and His consequent resurrection His life's purpose has been fulfilled. The lift that men need is the lift that the cross of Christ gives them. Being lifted up by the cross of Christ, they at the same time go down with Him into death and rise with Him to newness of life. That is the lift that Christianity offers to a confused and helpless world. The lift of the cross of Christ is the victory that overcomes the world. (1 John 5:4)

WHAT WILL DESTROY THE COLOSSUS?

Continued economic, technological, and military superiority will not necessarily destroy the colossus of communism. U. S. foreign aid running into billions of dollars annually may be helpful in containing our political or national enemies. But foreign aid coupled with the best of diplomacy will not secure for the church ascendancy in the non-Western world where religious and political leaders are now trying to revitalize the long slumbering national spirit through a revival and reinterpretation of Hinduism, Buddhism, and other ancient religious faiths. Although much must be said in favor of the church aligning itself with the cause of racial justice in the United States, the enactment of civil rights legislation and its implementation on all levels, the mere exercise of a humanitarian spirit on the part of Christian people will not give the church the lift it needs to make of it the dynamic powerhouse for the unity of God with man, and man with man, for the restoration of God's purpose in creation. If the organized church cannot act as the instrument of the Spirit of God, inculcating a faith that energizes men to work here and now for the unity of heaven and earth with all that such unity implies, as well as preparing them for a happy hereafter, what will be its future?

Fire for Judgment and Mercy

All signs seem to be pointing in one direction, to the destruction of the church as an institution, or to the end of the church as it is presently organized: the Roman Catholic Church, the Orthodox churches, the Lutheran Church, the Anglican Church, and the many Protestant church bodies—the Ecumenical Movement with all that it has in its favor notwithstanding. If this is to happen, communism, Asian and African nationalism, the resurgence of ancient non-Christian religions, and racism may be the instruments by which this cataclysmic happening will be brought about; but they will not be the ultimate cause. They will be the instruments of divine judgment—*fire from the throne* of God. Then divine mercy will reach down from heaven to pluck the church, the true bride of Christ, out of the dead ashes of the institution and give it new form and meaning in keeping with His still unrevealed purpose for the years that may lie ahead. The prophetic word of the one great Prophet, "I will build My church, and the powers of death shall not prevail against it" (Matt. 16:18), will be vindicated once again and most dramatically.

With the old form destroyed, what will be the new form in which the church will appear? What new form will God give it? The answer is the cross; that will be the church's simple form.

If Marxist and Leninist practitioners continue as God's unwitting servants, and others like Fidel Castro join them, and if the communist octopus takes us within its clutches—a not altogether impossible phenomenon—the church in this part of the world will be a church under the cross. And if that happens, if the greatest military power in the world, the United States, is "buried" as Nikita Khrushchev said it would be, and if faithful adherents to the communist ideology live out their religious convictions by dying for their god, the classless society—then the church, which is the one deadly foe of communism, will go underground, where the faithful of the communist party are in many lands today. The church under its new form will then be indeed what its Head promised it would be. It will be like the church of the Roman arena and the church of the catacombs. Christ will then have brought the church once again to where He said it would be, to that place where He Himself, the Suffering Servant of God, gave Himself as a sacrifice for the sins of the world, to a hill outside Jerusalem's walls where in Him death was "swallowed up in victory." (1 Cor. 15:54)

Fire from the throne of God is not all judgment; it is judgment so that mercy can come through.

If there is merit in the foregoing interpretation of the times in which we are now living and through which we are now passing, and if the true purpose of the judgment of God upon the church is understood and accepted, then there is also no reason for despair or hopelessness. The judgment is rather a sign that God has not abandoned His people. He is instead preparing them for the greatest era in history. By taking away that which they themselves had built up—the institution—He is preparing them to remember the source of their new strength, His new life which He alone supplies, and the form in which His church is to appear in the world—the form of a cross. And they are to remember the purpose of that new life made evident in that new form. That purpose is none other than His original and final purpose in dealing with men, the very purpose for which they were created, to live out their lives in unity with Him and their fellowman to the glory and praise of Him who created them. Then the words of St. Paul will not only make sense; they will take on new meaning: "It has been granted to you that for the sake of Christ you should not only believe in Him but also suffer for His sake." (Phil. 1:29)

Mingled with, or accompanied by, the fire of divine judgment is the fire of God's mercy that warms the heart and gives light for the journey through life. That fire is the Spirit of God, who imparts to men Christ, the God of all mercy, incarnate in the flesh of man. As Christ was about to make His appearance in His Messianic role, St. John the Baptist in preaching about Him referred to both fires from the throne of God, the fire of divine judgment and the fire that warms and gives light through divine mercy: "The axe is laid to the root of the trees; every tree therefore that does not bear good fruit is cut down and thrown into the fire. . . . But He who is coming . . . will baptize you with the Holy Spirit and with fire. His winnowing fork is in His hand, and He will clear His threshing floor and gather His wheat into the granary, but the chaff He will burn with unquenchable fire" (Matt. 3:10-12) – the fire of judgment and the fire of life, warmth, and light!

"He will baptize you with the Holy Spirit and with fire." And it happened. Ten days after His ascension, on the first Christian Pentecost day, His disciples miraculously experienced what John the Baptist had foretold: "There appeared to them tongues as of fire, distributed and resting on each one of them. And they were all filled with the Holy Spirit" (Acts 2:3-4). That event, symbolical of the life, warmth, and light that comes to man in Jesus Christ, marked the end of the old age and the beginning of the new.

The signs of the times seem to indicate clearly that the end of another age has come – "the dying of one world and, please God, the birth of a new one" – and with it not gloom and doom for God's people, but purpose and hope. If what is happening today in and to the church is thus interpreted, then the race issue is not only an expression of divine judgment upon an institution which is to be destroyed; it is also an indication, as someone has aptly said, that "God has chosen the race issue to purify the church."

But the race issue as it confronts our nation is not an entity of historical development somehow in isolation from what else is transpiring. It is rather an integral part of the whole world-engulfing revolution which points to the possible end of the political, social, and economic structure of modern society. If this takes place, and if a new structure is to rise out of the ashes of the old, who is to be its architect and builder?

As "we wait for new heavens and a new earth in which righteousness dwells" (2 Peter 3:13), we who are the church of Jesus Christ are not only to wait and to pray that the new structure be built to the glory of God; we are to participate in designing and building it. This is not idolatrous man-centeredness. It is precisely the opposite. For God in Christ has given to His people a new life, His life, so that His purpose in creation may be accomplished through them.

Notes

CHAPTER 1

1. John B. Morris, "Involved in Mankind," *On the Battle Lines*, ed. Malcolm Boyd (New York: Morehouse-Barlow Co., 1964), p. 84.
2. Press Release, Population Reference Bureau (Washington, D. C.), Jan. 16, 1967.
3. "World Population – 1963," in *Population Bulletin*, ed. Robert C. Cook (Washington, D. C.: Population Reference Bureau, Inc.), XIX, No. 6 (October 1963), 143.
4. See Ashley Montagu, *Man's Most Dangerous Myth: The Fallacy of Race* (Cleveland and New York: World Publishing Co., fourth rev. ed., 1964).
5. Anthony H. Richmond, *The Color Problem* (Baltimore: Penguin Books, 1955), pp. 13 – 14.
6. Ibid., p. 13.
7. See Ruth Benedict and Gene Weltfish, *The Races of Mankind* (New York: Public Affairs Committee), Public Affairs Pamphlet No. 85, July 1961.
8. Jessie Parkhurst Guzman, ed., *The Negro Year Book* (New York: Wm. H. Wise & Co., 1952), p. 1.
9. Lillian Smith, *Killers of the Dream* (New York: W. W. Norton & Co., 1961), pp. 34 – 38.

CHAPTER 2

1. See Kyle Haselden, *The Racial Problem in Christian Perspective* (New York: Harper & Bros., 1959), pp. 26 ff.
2. See Oscar Handlin, *Race and Nationality in American Life* (Boston: Little, Brown and Company, 1948), pp. 39 – 42.
3. Ibid., pp. 45 – 47.
4. See C. Vann Woodward, *The Strange Career of Jim Crow* (New York: Oxford University Press, Galaxy Book edition, 1957), pp. 45 ff.
5. "The failure of the churches at this point in our history [immediately preceding the Civil War] forced the country to turn to political action against slavery, and political action destroyed slavery as a system but left the hearts of the slaveholders unregenerate and left oppression of the free Negro little less of an evil than slavery had been." Dwight Lowell Dumond, *Antislavery – The Crusade for Freedom in America* (Ann Arbor: The University of Michigan Press, 1961), p. 344.
6. One might well assume that throughout the period of slavery and also after the Civil War, when segregation became the fixed way of life in Southern society, there were many people in the church who found the folkways into which they had been born somehow in contradiction with Christian faith and life. But being overwhelmed by the general acceptance of the system, both by the religious and secular forces surrounding them, they soon succumbed to the inevitable, and the call of the Christian conscience was lost in the loud cry of the many. There were, nevertheless, some courageous Christians who fought the system to the very end.
7. Wesley Shrader, "Segregation in the Churches," *Esquire*, May 1958, p. 120; emphasis added.
8. Joseph R. Washington, Jr., "Where Do We Go from Here in Campus Integration?" *Motive*, XXIII (January 1963), 26.

CHAPTER 3

1. In *Hound of Heaven* (New York: Dodd, Mead & Co.).

2. Vivian W. Henderson, *The Economic Status of Negroes: in the Nation and in the South,* pamphlet in the "Toward Regional Realism" Series, published by the Southern Regional Council, Sept. 1963, p. 5.
3. Ibid., p. 11.
4. Ibid., pp. 11–12.
5. While the decision was hailed throughout the world among the uncommitted nations as a victory for justice, the communist press, always ready to seize upon any opportunity to notify the nations of the world of our shortcomings, especially in the area of race relations, made but passing, insignificant reference to the historic decision.
6. An executive order issued in 1948 by President Harry S. Truman, calling for the elimination of segregation in the armed forces, was another significant step taken that helped to prepare the way for the sweeping changes that were soon to follow.
7. Daniel Bell, "The Dispossessed – 1962," *The Radical Right,* ed. Daniel Bell (Garden City, N. Y.: Doubleday & Company, Inc., 1963), p. 12.
8. Ibid., p. 19.
9. Ibid., p. 21.
10. Ibid., p. 34; emphasis added.
11. *Vital Speeches,* 30:647, Aug. 15, 1964.

CHAPTER 4

1. Martin H. Scharlemann, *Toward Tomorrow* (St. Louis: Concordia Publishing House, 1960), p. 8.
2. Kyle Haselden, *The Racial Problem in Christian Perspective* (New York: Harper & Bros., 1959), pp. 82–83.
3. Ibid., p. 76.
4. New York: Viking Press, 1955, p. 42.
5. July 10, 1964, p. 878.
6. E. g., Luke 8; Matt. 22; Luke 19:1-9; Matt. 5:20.
7. Anne Braden, *The Wall Between* (New York: Monthly Review Press, 1958), pp. 24–25.
8. In *The Screwtape Letters* by C. S. Lewis (New York: Macmillan, 1944, p. 37), Wormwood, the junior devil on earth, writes to Screwtape, the senior devil in hell. Wormwood has discovered conflicting emotions in those on earth among whom he is working – emotions of love and benevolence on the one hand, and malice and hatred on the other. Not knowing what to do, he asks Screwtape for advice. Back from the depths of hell comes the answer: "Do what you will, there is going to be some benevolence, as well as some malice, in your patient's soul. The great thing is to direct the malice to his immediate neighbours whom he meets every day and to thrust his benevolence out to the remote circumference, to people he does not know. The malice thus becomes wholly real and the benevolence largely imaginary."
9. New York: Macmillan, 1958.

CHAPTER 5

1. Though some sophisticates of the 20th century may find it difficult to see any relevance between the prophecy of Ezekiel and the race issue, the illiterate Negro slaves on the Southern plantations were able to do so. And because of their insight we have the spiritual "Dry Bones."
2. "I Sold a House to a Negro," *Ebony,* October 1963.
3. Sermons from the Year 1535, *D. Martin Luthers Werke,* XLI (Weimar: Hermann Boehlaus, 1905), 303; as translated by Margarete Steiner and Percy Scott in *Day by Day We Magnify Thee* (Philadelphia: Muhlenberg Press, 1950), p. 419.
4. *The Fire Next Time* (New York: Dial Press, 1963), pp. 112–13.

5. "The man who suffered the wrong is the man to demand redress . . . the man struck is the man to cry out . . . he who has endured the cruel pangs of slavery is the man to advocate liberty." Frederick Douglass, as quoted in *Before the Mayflower,* by Lerone Bennett, Jr. (Chicago: Johnson Publishing Company, 1963), p. 149.
6. *Strength to Love* (New York: Harper & Row, 1964), p. 40.

CHAPTER 6

1. Bernard Iddings Bell (New York: Harper & Brothers, 1945), pp. 81, 74.
2. Arna Bontemps, *100 Years of Negro Freedom* (New York: Dodd, Mead & Co., 1961), p. 243; emphasis added.
3. Ruth Cranston, *World Faiths* (New York: Harper & Brothers, 1949).

CHAPTER 7

1. *Concordia or Book of Concord* (St. Louis: Concordia Publishing House, 1957), p. 186; emphasis added.
2. Schrey, Walz, and Whitehouse, *The Biblical Doctrine of Justice and Law,* Ecumenical Biblical Studies No. 3 (published for the Division of Studies, World Council of Churches, by SCM Press Ltd., London, 1950), pp. 124–25, 141, 146–47; emphasis added.
3. The distinguished author, Christian humanitarian, and lay polemicist Alan Paton wrote two articles published in *The Christian Century.* Feb. 26 (pp. 248–49) and March 5, 1958 (pp. 278–80), issues; both of them treat with clarity and in true theological perspective the subject discussed here. What he calls the supratemporal goods of creation is what I have in mind in the phrase "the psychic stuff of creation."
4. "In the economic and social order there are persons who are the principle bearers or agents in unjust practices and who are close material cooperators in that injustice. These may have to be directly coerced in the struggle for justice, since pressures brought to bear upon them may be the only way to attack the impacted, customary injustice that should be resisted and changed for the sake of fellow humanity. The economic boycott of their segregated businesses; picket lines of protests in front of their stores to arouse the community, to induce people not to trade with them, and to compel them to change their policies: these things are quite in order." Paul Ramsey, *Christian Ethics and the Sit-in* (New York: Association Press, 1961), p. 105.
5. In his "Letter from Birmingham City Jail," Martin Luther King, Jr., writes: "In no sense do I advocate evading or defying the law as the rabid segregationist would do. This would lead to anarchy. One who breaks an unjust law must do it *openly, lovingly* (not hatefully as the white mothers did in New Orleans when they were seen on television screaming 'nigger, nigger, nigger') and with a willingness to accept the penalty. I submit that an individual who breaks a law that conscience tells him is unjust, and willingly accepts the penalty by staying in jail to arouse the conscience of the community over its injustice, is in reality expressing the very highest respect for law." P. 7 of pamphlet publication of the Letter by the American Friends Service Committee.
6. For several examples of civil disobedience in the Old Testament, see Dan. 1, 3, and 6; Ex. 2.
7. Gerhard Ebeling, *Word and Faith* (Philadelphia: Fortress Press, 1963), p. 392.

CHAPTER 8

1. *An American Dilemma* (New York: Harper & Brothers, 1944), I, 55.
2. Gordon W. Allport, *The Nature of Prejudice* (Garden City, N. Y.: Doubleday Anchor Books, 1958), p. 23.
3. Fred D. Wentzel, *Epistle to White Christians* (Philadelphia and St. Louis: Christian Education Press, 1948), p. 7; emphasis added.

4. *An American Dilemma,* I, 60 ff.
5. Paul G. Hansen, "Interracial Marriage," *Arena,* LXXII: 6 (February 1964), 20–21.
6. On June 12, 1967, the U.S. Supreme Court handed down a decision declaring anti-interracial-marriage laws unconstitutional.
7. William D. Workman, Jr., *The Case for the South* (New York: The Devin-Adair Co., 1960), pp. 218–19.
8. "Marriage Is Honorable in All," *Interracial Marriage?* Proceedings of the Valparaiso University Institute on Human Relations, July 25–27, 1958 (Valparaiso, Ind.: Lutheran Human Relations Association of America, 1958), p. 33.
9. Milton Mayer, "The Issue Is Miscegenation," *The Progressive,* XXIII, 9 (September 1959), 9.
10. Markus Barth, "Marriage Is Not the Chief End of Man," *Social Progress,* I, 4 (February 1960), 7.
11. "Marriage Is Honorable in All," p. 33.

Chapter 9

1. See Thomas Coates, "The Communion of Saints," *Proceedings, Valparaiso University Institute on Human Relations* (Valparaiso, Ind.: Lutheran Human Relations Association of America, 1957), p. 20.
2. Richard R. Caemmerer, *The Church in the World,* 3d print., rev., Concord Books (St. Louis: Concordia, 1961), p. 80.
3. Allan Galloway, *The Cosmic Christ* (New York: Harper & Bros., 1951), p. 232.

Chapter 10

1. J. H. Oldham, *The Oxford Conference—Official Report* (Chicago, New York: Willett, Clark & Co., 1937), p. 2.
2. See Anson Phelps Stokes, *Church and State in the United States* (New York: Harper & Bros., 1950), II, 380; *The Christian Century,* LIV (Aug. 18, 1937), 1017; ibid. (Oct. 20, 1937), 1292; Norman Goodall, *The Ecumenical Movement: What It Is and What It Does* (London: Oxford University Press, 1961), pp. 63–68.
3. Oldham, pp. 213–14, 216.
4. Is it altogether unlikely that Pope Pius XII was influenced at least in part by the Oxford Conference when he included the following statement in his *Summi Pontificatus* (1939)? He spoke of "a marvelous vision which makes us see the human race in the unity of one common origin in God, 'one God and Father of all, who is above all and in us all' (Eph. 4:6); in the unity of human nature, which in every man is equally composed of material body and spiritual, immortal soul; in the unity of the immediate end and mission in the world; in the unity of dwelling place, the earth, of whose resources all men by natural right avail themselves to sustain life and develop life; in the unity of the supernatural end, God Himself, to whom all should tend in the unity of means to secure that end." John LaFarge, *The Catholic Viewpoint on Race Relations* (Garden City, N.Y.: Hanover House, 1956), p. 83.

   A parallel: The late Cardinal Ritter of St. Louis, upon his return from the first session of the Second Vatican Council, is quoted as having said: "I suspect Pope John's inspiration to call the Second Vatican Council came from heaven in part via the World Council of Churches." William J. Danker, *Two Worlds or None: Rediscovering Missions* (St. Louis: Concordia Publishing House, 1964), p. 44.
5. As quoted in Anson Phelps Stokes, II, 381–82; emphasis added.
6. John LaFarge, *The Catholic Viewpoint on Race Relations* (Garden City, N.Y.: Hanover House, 1956), p. 70.
7. Bill Andrews, "Race Relations: Society for Unity," *The Living Church,* CX 4, 2 (Jan. 10, 1960), 6; emphasis added.
8. Fred H. Lindemann, *The Sermon and the Propers,* II (St. Louis: Concordia Publishing House, 1958), 214.
9. Franklin H. Littell, "The Recovery of Ministry," in Ecumenical Institute *Newsletter*

(Church Federation of Greater Chicago), I, 2 (June 1964), 1.

10. *Encyclopedia of Religion,* ed. Vergilius Ferm (Paterson, N. J.: Littlefield, Adams & Co., 1959), p. 445.
11. Michael J. Taylor, S. J., *The Protestant Liturgical Renewal—a Catholic Viewpoint* (Westminster, Md.: The Newman Press, 1963), p. 4; emphasis added.
12. Ibid., p. xvi.
13. Ibid., p. 34.
14. E. Franklin Frazier, *The Negro Church in America* (New York: Schocken Books, 1963), pp. 43–44.
15. From the Episcopal Address delivered at the Methodist General Conference, April 26, 1965. ("The Episcopal Address, while written by one man, is the united word of the Council of Bishops of the Methodist Church.") *Daily Christian Advocate,* Proceedings of the General Conference of The Methodist Church, VII (1), April 27, 1964, 15–16.
16. William J. Danker, *Two Worlds or None* (St. Louis: Concordia Publishing House, 1964), p. 38.

Chapter 11

1. R. Pierce Beaver, "The Readiness of the World for the Mission" (essay delivered at the Study Conference on the Christian World Mission, conducted under the auspices of Concordia Seminary, St. Louis, Mo., Oct. 11–13, 1961), p. 5, mimeographed.
2. Robert Scharlemann, *Communism and the Christian Faith* (St. Louis: Concordia Publishing House, 1963), p. 13.
3. A further service that Christian anticommunists are rendering the communist cause is to awaken doubt and suspicion as to the integrity of our own governmental officials. For "it is standard Communist procedure to sow seeds of doubt and suspicion against the government and its leaders in a country scheduled for take-over. How far this process has advanced in the United States is indicated in the following paragraph from the *Literary Gazette* of Moscow, dated April 4, 1961, in an article in the Russian language: 'The predictions of Lenin are materializing . . . in the United States. . . . Lenin said that the most ardent foes of communism will eventually become frightened and suspicious of anybody who does not agree with them. In this manner these extremely nationalistic capitalists will actually work for the cause of communism by eliminating some of the largest obstacles on the road toward a worldwide Communist way of life.'" ("Sowing Dissension in the Churches," published by The National Council, Episcopal Church Center, 815 Second Ave., New York, N. Y., mimeographed, p. 24.)
4. Elton Trueblood, *Alternative to Futility* (New York and London: Harper & Bros., 1948), pp. 25–26.

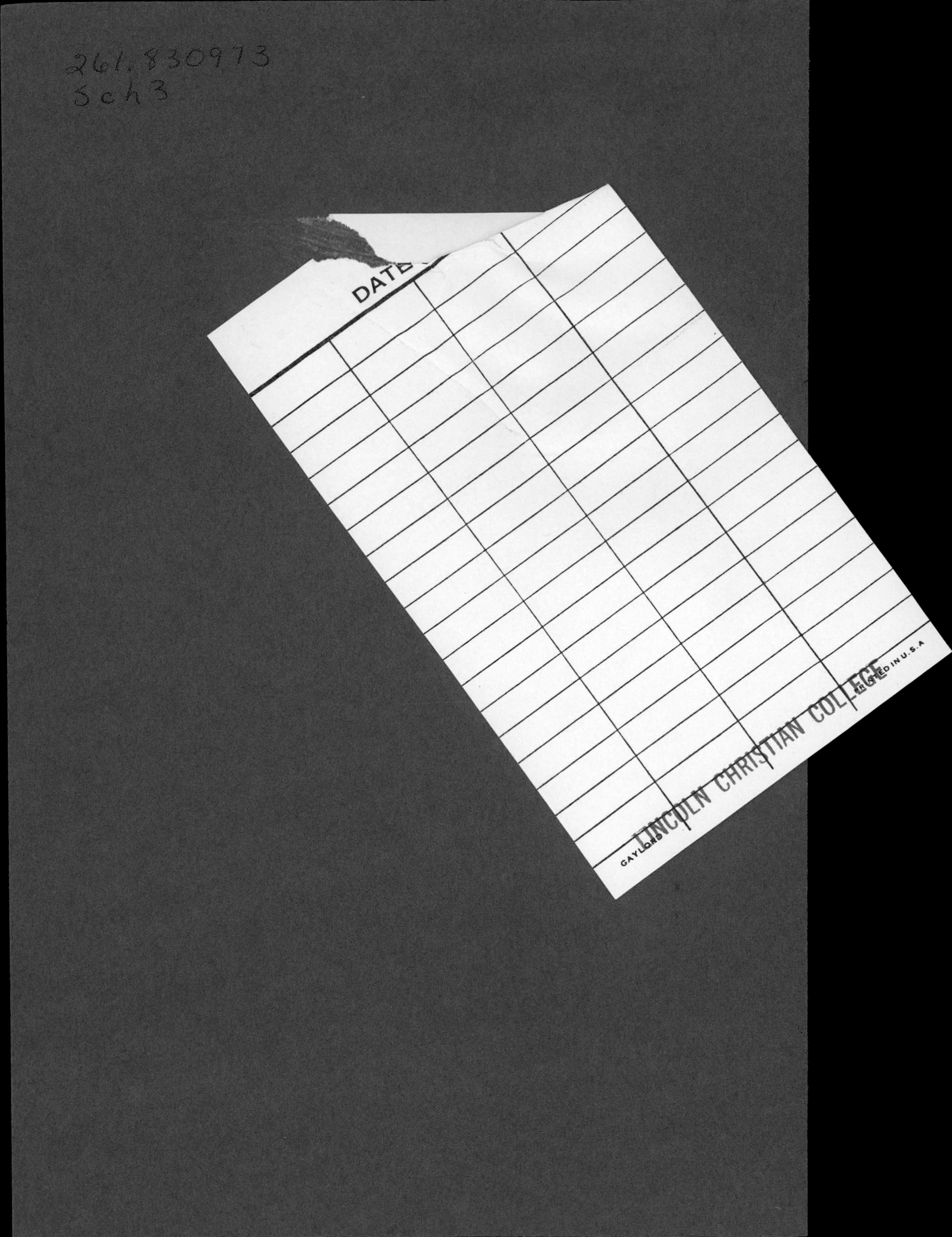
DATE
GAYLORD
PRINTED IN U.S.A.